50 Australian Dinner Food Recipes for Home

By: Kelly Johnson

Table of Contents

- Avocado Toast
- Smashed Peas on Toast
- Bacon and Egg Roll
- Vegemite on Toast
- Pancakes with Maple Syrup
- Fruit Salad with Yogurt
- Bircher Muesli
- Acai Bowl
- Grilled Tomato and Mushroom Breakfast
- Australian-style French Toast
- Egg and Bacon Pie
- Pikelets (Mini Pancakes)
- Anzac Biscuits
- Lamingtons
- Sausage Rolls
- Damper (Australian Soda Bread)
- Chia Pudding
- Ricotta Hotcakes
- Corn Fritters
- Beetroot and Sweet Potato Hash
- Australian Beef Sausage
- Sautéed Spinach and Mushrooms
- Zucchini and Sweet Corn Fritters
- Australian-Style Scones with Jam and Cream
- Pumpkin and Ricotta Pancakes
- Croissants with Ham and Cheese
- Breakfast Burrito
- Aussie Meat Pie
- Baked Beans on Toast
- Cherry Ripe Slice
- Caramel Slice
- Egg White Omelette
- Chocolate Lamingtons
- Sourdough Toast with Vegemite
- Aussie Breakfast Pizza
- Veggie Frittata

- Grilled Haloumi with Avocado
- Vegemite and Cheese Scrolls
- Beef Sausage Rolls
- Aussie BBQ Breakfast
- Banana Bread with Macadamia Nuts
- Salted Caramel Tim Tam Slice
- Lemon Myrtle and Aniseed Myrtle Granola
- Aussie Bacon and Egg Pie
- Aussie Hash Browns
- Aussie Weet-Bix Slice
- Aussie Pumpkin Bread
- Aussie Gluten-Free Bread
- Aussie Zucchini Bread
- Aussie Orange Marmalade

Avocado Toast

Ingredients:

- 2 slices of bread (sourdough, whole grain, or your preference)
- 1 ripe avocado
- Salt and pepper, to taste
- Red pepper flakes (optional)
- Lemon juice (optional)
- Cherry tomatoes, sliced (optional)
- Fresh herbs (such as cilantro or parsley), chopped (optional)
- Poached or fried egg (optional, for added protein)

Instructions:

1. **Prepare the Avocado:**
   - Cut the avocado in half, remove the pit, and scoop the flesh into a bowl.
2. **Mash the Avocado:**
   - Use a fork to mash the avocado until smooth or slightly chunky, depending on your preference.
3. **Season the Avocado:**
   - Season with salt and pepper to taste. You can also add a squeeze of lemon juice for brightness and a pinch of red pepper flakes for heat.
4. **Toast the Bread:**
   - Toast the bread slices until golden brown and crispy.
5. **Assemble the Avocado Toast:**
   - Spread the mashed avocado evenly onto the toasted bread slices.
6. **Add Toppings (Optional):**
   - Sprinkle with sliced cherry tomatoes, fresh herbs, or add a poached or fried egg on top for extra flavor and protein.
7. **Serve:**
   - Enjoy your avocado toast immediately while the bread is still warm and crispy.

Avocado toast is versatile, satisfying, and can be customized with various toppings to suit your taste preferences. It's a nutritious and delicious way to start your day!

Smashed Peas on Toast

Ingredients:

- 1 cup frozen peas
- 1 tbsp olive oil
- 1-2 cloves garlic, minced
- Salt and pepper, to taste
- Squeeze of lemon juice (optional)
- 2 slices of bread (sourdough, whole grain, or your choice)
- Optional toppings: crumbled feta cheese, fresh herbs (such as mint or parsley), sliced avocado

Instructions:

1. **Cook the Peas:**
   - Bring a small pot of water to a boil. Add the frozen peas and cook for about 2-3 minutes, until tender. Drain and set aside.
2. **Smash the Peas:**
   - In a bowl, add the cooked peas along with olive oil, minced garlic, salt, and pepper. Use a fork or potato masher to smash the peas until they are partially mashed but still have some texture. If desired, add a squeeze of lemon juice for brightness.
3. **Toast the Bread:**
   - Toast the bread slices until golden brown and crispy.
4. **Assemble the Smashed Peas on Toast:**
   - Spread the smashed peas mixture evenly onto the toasted bread slices.
5. **Add Toppings (Optional):**
   - Sprinkle with crumbled feta cheese, fresh herbs, or sliced avocado for additional flavor and texture.
6. **Serve:**
   - Enjoy your smashed peas on toast immediately while the bread is warm and crispy.

This dish is not only delicious but also packed with fiber and nutrients from the peas, making it a healthy and satisfying breakfast option.

Bacon and Egg Roll

Ingredients:

- 2-4 slices of bacon (depending on how much bacon you prefer)
- 2 eggs
- 2 soft bread rolls (or hamburger buns)
- Butter or oil, for cooking
- Salt and pepper, to taste
- Optional toppings: sliced cheese, avocado, tomato, lettuce, barbecue sauce

Instructions:

1. **Cook the Bacon:**
   - Heat a skillet or frying pan over medium heat. Add the bacon slices and cook until crispy, flipping occasionally. Once cooked to your liking, remove the bacon from the pan and drain on paper towels.
2. **Cook the Eggs:**
   - In the same skillet or frying pan (you can use the bacon fat or add a little butter/oil), crack the eggs and cook them sunny-side up or to your preference (fried, scrambled, or poached).
3. **Prepare the Rolls:**
   - While the eggs are cooking, lightly toast the bread rolls in a toaster or under a grill until warmed and slightly crispy.
4. **Assemble the Bacon and Egg Rolls:**
   - Spread a little butter on each side of the toasted rolls.
   - Layer the cooked bacon slices on the bottom half of each roll.
   - Place the cooked eggs on top of the bacon.
   - Season with salt and pepper, to taste.
5. **Add Optional Toppings (if desired):**
   - Add sliced cheese, avocado slices, tomato, lettuce, or a drizzle of barbecue sauce for extra flavor.
6. **Serve:**
   - Close the rolls and serve immediately while warm. Enjoy your delicious Bacon and Egg Roll!

This recipe is straightforward and can be customized to suit your taste preferences. It's a perfect breakfast option for a hearty start to the day or a satisfying brunch.

Vegemite on Toast

Ingredients:

- Slices of bread (sourdough, whole grain, or your preference)
- Butter or margarine (optional)
- Vegemite

Instructions:

1. **Toast the Bread:**
    - Toast the bread slices until they are golden brown and crispy.
2. **Spread Vegemite:**
    - While the toast is still warm, spread a thin layer of Vegemite over the entire surface of each slice. The amount of Vegemite used can vary based on personal preference, but start with a small amount and add more as desired.
3. **Optional: Add Butter or Margarine:**
    - Some people like to spread a thin layer of butter or margarine on the toast before adding Vegemite. This step is optional and depends on personal taste.
4. **Serve:**
    - Serve the Vegemite toast immediately while it is still warm and crispy. It pairs well with a cup of coffee or tea.

Tips for Enjoying Vegemite on Toast:

- **Start with a Small Amount:** Vegemite has a strong flavor, so it's best to start with a thin layer and adjust to taste.
- **Experiment with Toppings:** If desired, you can top Vegemite toast with avocado slices, tomato, cheese, or a poached egg for added flavor and texture.
- **Store Vegemite Properly:** Keep Vegemite stored in a cool, dry place and tightly sealed to maintain freshness.

Vegemite on toast is a quick and easy breakfast option that's loved by many Australians for its unique and savory taste.

Pancakes with Maple Syrup

Ingredients:

- 1 cup all-purpose flour
- 2 tbsp granulated sugar
- 1 tsp baking powder
- 1/2 tsp baking soda
- 1/4 tsp salt
- 3/4 cup buttermilk (or substitute with milk mixed with 1 tbsp vinegar or lemon juice)
- 1/4 cup milk
- 1 large egg
- 2 tbsp unsalted butter, melted
- 1 tsp vanilla extract (optional)
- Butter or oil, for cooking
- Maple syrup, for serving

Instructions:

1. **Prepare the Batter:**
    - In a mixing bowl, whisk together the flour, sugar, baking powder, baking soda, and salt.
2. **Mix Wet Ingredients:**
    - In another bowl, whisk together the buttermilk, milk, egg, melted butter, and vanilla extract (if using).
3. **Combine Ingredients:**
    - Pour the wet ingredients into the dry ingredients and gently mix until just combined. Be careful not to overmix; it's okay if the batter is slightly lumpy.
4. **Heat the Griddle or Pan:**
    - Heat a non-stick griddle or large skillet over medium heat. Add a small amount of butter or oil and spread it evenly.
5. **Cook the Pancakes:**
    - Pour about 1/4 cup of batter onto the hot griddle for each pancake. Cook until bubbles form on the surface of the pancake and the edges look set, about 2-3 minutes.
6. **Flip and Cook:**
    - Carefully flip the pancake with a spatula and cook until the other side is golden brown, about 1-2 minutes more.
7. **Serve:**
    - Transfer the cooked pancakes to a plate and keep warm. Repeat with the remaining batter, adding more butter or oil to the griddle as needed.
8. **Serve with Maple Syrup:**
    - Stack the pancakes on plates and drizzle generously with maple syrup. Optionally, top with a pat of butter before serving.

Tips for Perfect Pancakes:

- **Use Buttermilk:** If possible, use buttermilk or a substitute (milk with vinegar or lemon juice) for extra fluffy pancakes.
- **Don't Overmix:** Mix the batter until just combined; overmixing can result in tough pancakes.
- **Adjust Heat:** Adjust the heat as needed to ensure pancakes cook evenly without burning.

Enjoy your delicious pancakes with maple syrup for a comforting and satisfying breakfast or brunch!

Fruit Salad with Yogurt

Ingredients:

- Assorted fresh fruits (such as strawberries, blueberries, raspberries, blackberries, pineapple, kiwi, mango, grapes, etc.), washed, peeled, and chopped as needed
- 1 cup plain Greek yogurt (or any yogurt of your choice)
- 1-2 tbsp honey (optional, for sweetness)
- Fresh mint leaves, chopped (optional, for garnish)

Instructions:

1. **Prepare the Fruits:**
   - Wash and prepare the fruits by chopping them into bite-sized pieces. Use a variety of fruits for color and flavor.
2. **Mix the Yogurt:**
   - In a mixing bowl, stir the plain Greek yogurt until smooth. If desired, mix in honey to sweeten the yogurt to your taste.
3. **Assemble the Fruit Salad:**
   - Combine the chopped fruits in a large bowl.
4. **Serve:**
   - Divide the mixed fruits into individual serving bowls or plates.
5. **Add Yogurt:**
   - Spoon a generous dollop of yogurt over each serving of fruit salad.
6. **Garnish (Optional):**
   - Garnish with fresh mint leaves for a burst of freshness.
7. **Enjoy:**
   - Serve the fruit salad with yogurt immediately and enjoy the delicious combination of fresh fruits and creamy yogurt.

Tips for Making Fruit Salad with Yogurt:

- **Use Fresh and Ripe Fruits:** Choose a variety of fruits that are in season and ripe for the best flavor.
- **Customize:** Feel free to customize your fruit salad with additional toppings such as nuts, granola, or a sprinkle of cinnamon.
- **Make Ahead:** You can prepare the fruit salad and yogurt separately ahead of time and combine them just before serving to keep the fruits fresh.

This fruit salad with yogurt is not only delicious but also packed with vitamins, minerals, and probiotics from the yogurt, making it a healthy and satisfying breakfast or snack option.

Bircher Muesli

Ingredients:

- 1 cup rolled oats (not instant oats)
- 1 cup milk (dairy milk, almond milk, or any milk of your choice)
- 1/2 cup plain Greek yogurt
- 1 apple, grated (with skin on)
- 1/4 cup nuts (such as almonds, walnuts, or hazelnuts), chopped
- 2 tbsp honey or maple syrup (optional, for sweetness)
- 1/2 tsp vanilla extract
- 1/4 tsp ground cinnamon (optional)
- Fresh fruits (such as berries, bananas, or kiwi), sliced or chopped, for topping
- Additional toppings: dried fruits, seeds (chia seeds, flaxseeds), coconut flakes

Instructions:

1. **Combine Ingredients:**
   - In a large mixing bowl, combine the rolled oats, milk, Greek yogurt, grated apple, chopped nuts, honey or maple syrup (if using), vanilla extract, and ground cinnamon (if using). Stir until well combined.
2. **Mix and Chill:**
   - Cover the bowl with plastic wrap or a lid and refrigerate for at least 2 hours or overnight. This allows the oats to soften and absorb the flavors.
3. **Serve:**
   - Before serving, give the Bircher muesli a good stir. If it's too thick, you can add a splash of milk to reach your desired consistency.
4. **Top with Fruits and Enjoy:**
   - Divide the Bircher muesli into serving bowls and top with fresh fruits and any additional toppings you like, such as dried fruits, seeds, or coconut flakes.
5. **Optional: Drizzle with Honey or Maple Syrup:**
   - For extra sweetness, drizzle a little honey or maple syrup over the top of each serving.
6. **Enjoy Your Bircher Muesli:**
   - Serve chilled and enjoy your creamy and nutritious Bircher muesli for breakfast or as a refreshing snack.

Tips for Making Bircher Muesli:

- **Grate the Apple:** Grating the apple with the skin on adds natural sweetness and texture to the muesli.
- **Customize:** Feel free to customize your Bircher muesli with your favorite fruits, nuts, and toppings.

- **Make Ahead:** Bircher muesli can be made the night before and stored in the refrigerator for up to 2-3 days. It's a convenient breakfast option for busy mornings.

Bircher muesli is not only delicious but also packed with fiber, protein, and vitamins from the oats, yogurt, fruits, and nuts, making it a healthy and filling breakfast choice.

Acai Bowl

Ingredients:

- 2 packs of frozen acai berry puree (unsweetened, available in health food stores or online)
- 1 banana, sliced (plus extra for topping)
- 1/2 cup mixed berries (such as strawberries, blueberries, raspberries)
- 1/2 cup unsweetened almond milk (or any milk of your choice)
- 1 tbsp honey or maple syrup (optional, for sweetness)
- Toppings: granola, sliced fruits (such as banana, berries, kiwi), shredded coconut, chia seeds, hemp seeds, nuts (such as almonds, walnuts)

Instructions:

1. **Blend the Acai Bowl Base:**
   - In a blender, combine the frozen acai berry puree, sliced banana, mixed berries, almond milk, and honey or maple syrup (if using). Blend until smooth and creamy. You may need to stop and stir occasionally to help the blending process.
2. **Prepare the Toppings:**
   - While the acai mixture is blending, prepare your desired toppings. Slice additional fruits, measure out granola, and gather any other toppings you want to use.
3. **Assemble the Acai Bowl:**
   - Pour the blended acai mixture into a bowl.
4. **Add Toppings:**
   - Arrange the toppings on top of the acai mixture. Start with a generous sprinkle of granola, then add sliced fruits, shredded coconut, chia seeds, hemp seeds, and nuts.
5. **Serve:**
   - Enjoy your Acai Bowl immediately with a spoon. It's best enjoyed cold and fresh.

Tips for Making Acai Bowl:

- **Frozen Acai Puree:** Make sure to use unsweetened frozen acai berry puree for the best flavor and nutrition.
- **Customize:** Feel free to customize your Acai Bowl with your favorite fruits, nuts, seeds, and granola.
- **Texture:** The consistency should be thick enough to eat with a spoon but smooth enough to blend easily.

Acai bowls are not only delicious but also packed with antioxidants, fiber, and essential nutrients from the fruits and toppings, making them a nutritious and satisfying breakfast option.

Grilled Tomato and Mushroom Breakfast

Ingredients:

- 2 large tomatoes, sliced thickly
- 1 cup button mushrooms, sliced
- 2 tbsp olive oil
- Salt and pepper, to taste
- 1-2 cloves garlic, minced (optional)
- Fresh herbs (such as parsley or thyme), chopped, for garnish
- Toasted bread or toast, to serve

Instructions:

1. **Prepare the Vegetables:**
   - Heat a grill pan or skillet over medium-high heat. Brush the tomato slices and mushroom slices with olive oil on both sides.
2. **Grill the Tomatoes and Mushrooms:**
   - Place the tomato slices on the grill pan and cook for about 3-4 minutes on each side, until grill marks appear and the tomatoes soften slightly. Remove from the pan and set aside.
   - In the same pan, add the sliced mushrooms. Cook for about 5-7 minutes, stirring occasionally, until the mushrooms are tender and lightly browned. If using minced garlic, add it to the mushrooms during the last minute of cooking.
3. **Season:**
   - Season the grilled tomatoes and mushrooms with salt and pepper to taste.
4. **Assemble the Breakfast:**
   - Arrange the grilled tomatoes and mushrooms on a serving plate.
5. **Garnish and Serve:**
   - Garnish with chopped fresh herbs, such as parsley or thyme.
6. **Serve with Toast:**
   - Serve the grilled tomato and mushroom breakfast with toasted bread or toast on the side.

Tips for Grilled Tomato and Mushroom Breakfast:

- **Variations:** You can add other vegetables like bell peppers or zucchini to the grill for additional flavor and texture.
- **Herbs:** Experiment with different herbs like basil or rosemary for added freshness.
- **Protein:** Consider adding a poached or fried egg on top for extra protein and to make it a more substantial meal.

This grilled tomato and mushroom breakfast is not only delicious but also a healthy choice packed with vitamins and minerals. It's perfect for those looking for a savory breakfast option to start their day right.

Australian-style French Toast

Ingredients:

- 4 slices of thick-cut bread (such as brioche, sourdough, or white bread)
- 2 large eggs
- 1/2 cup milk (dairy or plant-based)
- 1 tsp vanilla extract
- 1/2 tsp ground cinnamon
- Butter or oil, for cooking
- Maple syrup, for serving
- Fresh berries or sliced fruits, for serving (optional)

Instructions:

1. **Prepare the Bread:**
   - If using thick-cut bread, slice it into slices about 1 inch thick. This helps the bread soak up the egg mixture without becoming too soggy.
2. **Mix the Egg Mixture:**
   - In a shallow bowl or baking dish, whisk together the eggs, milk, vanilla extract, and ground cinnamon until well combined.
3. **Soak the Bread:**
   - Dip each slice of bread into the egg mixture, ensuring both sides are coated evenly. Allow the bread to soak for about 20-30 seconds on each side, depending on the thickness of your bread.
4. **Cook the French Toast:**
   - Heat a large skillet or griddle over medium heat and add a pat of butter or a drizzle of oil to coat the surface.
   - Carefully place the soaked bread slices onto the skillet or griddle. Cook for about 2-3 minutes on each side, or until golden brown and cooked through. Adjust the heat as needed to prevent burning.
5. **Serve:**
   - Transfer the cooked French toast to serving plates.
6. **Garnish and Serve:**
   - Serve warm with a drizzle of maple syrup and fresh berries or sliced fruits, if desired.

Tips for Making Australian-style French Toast:

- **Bread Selection:** Choose a bread with good structure, like brioche or sourdough, which holds up well to soaking and cooking.
- **Flavor Variations:** You can add a pinch of nutmeg or a splash of orange juice to the egg mixture for added flavor.

- **Keep Warm:** If making multiple batches, keep cooked French toast warm in a low oven (around 200°F or 90°C) while you finish cooking the rest.

Australian-style French toast is a delightful breakfast treat that's perfect for leisurely mornings or special occasions. Enjoy its fluffy texture and sweet flavors with your favorite toppings!

Egg and Bacon Pie

Ingredients:

- 1 sheet of ready-rolled shortcrust pastry (store-bought or homemade)
- 6 eggs
- 200g bacon, diced
- 1 cup grated cheese (cheddar or mozzarella)
- 1/2 cup milk or cream
- Salt and pepper, to taste
- Optional: chopped fresh herbs (such as parsley or chives)
- Butter or oil, for greasing

Instructions:

1. **Prepare the Pastry:**
   - Preheat your oven to 180°C (350°F). Lightly grease a pie dish with butter or oil.
   - Line the pie dish with the shortcrust pastry, pressing it gently into the corners and trimming any excess around the edges.
2. **Cook the Bacon:**
   - In a frying pan, cook the diced bacon over medium heat until crispy. Drain on paper towels to remove excess grease.
3. **Prepare the Filling:**
   - In a bowl, whisk together the eggs and milk or cream. Season with salt and pepper to taste. Stir in the grated cheese, cooked bacon, and chopped fresh herbs if using.
4. **Assemble and Bake:**
   - Pour the egg mixture into the prepared pastry-lined pie dish.
5. **Bake the Pie:**
   - Place the pie dish in the preheated oven and bake for 30-35 minutes, or until the filling is set and the pastry is golden brown.
6. **Serve:**
   - Remove the Egg and Bacon Pie from the oven and let it cool slightly before slicing and serving.

Tips for Making Egg and Bacon Pie:

- **Variations:** You can add other ingredients to the filling, such as diced vegetables (like onions or spinach), cooked sausage, or herbs for extra flavor.
- **Pastry Options:** If you prefer a puff pastry crust, you can use that instead of shortcrust pastry for a lighter texture.
- **Make Ahead:** You can prepare the pie ahead of time and bake it just before serving. It also stores well in the refrigerator and can be reheated.

Egg and Bacon Pie is a hearty and delicious dish that's perfect for gatherings or a comforting meal at home. Enjoy it warm or at room temperature with a side salad for a complete meal!

Pikelets (Mini Pancakes)

Ingredients:

- 1 cup self-raising flour
- 1 tbsp sugar
- 1/2 tsp baking powder
- Pinch of salt
- 3/4 cup milk
- 1 large egg
- Butter or oil, for cooking

Instructions:

1. **Prepare the Batter:**
    - In a mixing bowl, sift together the self-raising flour, sugar, baking powder, and salt.
2. **Mix Wet Ingredients:**
    - In another bowl, whisk together the milk and egg until well combined.
3. **Combine Ingredients:**
    - Gradually pour the milk and egg mixture into the dry ingredients, stirring gently until smooth. The batter should be thick but pourable. If it's too thick, you can add a little more milk.
4. **Heat the Pan:**
    - Heat a non-stick frying pan or griddle over medium heat. Add a small amount of butter or oil and spread it evenly.
5. **Cook the Pikelets:**
    - Spoon about 2 tablespoons of batter onto the hot pan for each pikelet. You can cook several pikelets at a time, depending on the size of your pan.
6. **Cook Until Bubbles Form:**
    - Cook the pikelets for about 1-2 minutes, or until bubbles start to form on the surface and the edges look set.
7. **Flip and Cook the Other Side:**
    - Carefully flip the pikelets with a spatula and cook for another 1-2 minutes, or until golden brown and cooked through.
8. **Keep Warm:**
    - Transfer the cooked pikelets to a plate and cover with a clean kitchen towel to keep them warm while you cook the remaining batter.
9. **Serve:**
    - Serve the pikelets warm with your choice of toppings, such as butter, jam, honey, maple syrup, or fresh fruits.

Tips for Making Pikelets:

- **Consistency:** The batter should be thick enough to hold its shape but still spread slightly when spooned onto the pan.
- **Cooking Temperature:** Adjust the heat as needed to ensure the pikelets cook evenly without burning.
- **Variations:** You can add vanilla extract or lemon zest to the batter for added flavor, or fold in blueberries or chocolate chips for extra indulgence.

Pikelets are perfect for breakfast or as a sweet treat for morning or afternoon tea. They are versatile and can be enjoyed with a variety of toppings to suit your taste preferences.

Anzac Biscuits

Ingredients:

- 1 cup rolled oats
- 1 cup desiccated coconut
- 1 cup all-purpose flour
- 1 cup brown sugar
- 125g (1/2 cup + 1 tbsp) unsalted butter
- 2 tbsp golden syrup (or substitute with honey or corn syrup)
- 1 tsp baking soda
- 2 tbsp boiling water

Instructions:

1. **Preheat Oven and Prepare Baking Sheet:**
   - Preheat your oven to 160°C (320°F) and line a baking sheet with parchment paper.
2. **Mix Dry Ingredients:**
   - In a large bowl, combine the rolled oats, desiccated coconut, all-purpose flour, and brown sugar. Mix well to combine.
3. **Melt Butter and Syrup:**
   - In a small saucepan, melt the unsalted butter together with the golden syrup over low heat until smooth and well combined.
4. **Mix Baking Soda and Water:**
   - In a small bowl, dissolve the baking soda in the boiling water.
5. **Combine Wet and Dry Ingredients:**
   - Pour the melted butter and syrup mixture into the dry ingredients. Add the dissolved baking soda and water mixture. Stir until all ingredients are well combined and the mixture forms a sticky dough.
6. **Form Biscuits:**
   - Take tablespoonfuls of the mixture and roll into balls. Place them onto the lined baking sheet, leaving some space between each one. Flatten each ball slightly with the back of a fork.
7. **Bake:**
   - Bake in the preheated oven for 12-15 minutes, or until the biscuits are golden brown.
8. **Cool and Serve:**
   - Allow the Anzac biscuits to cool on the baking sheet for a few minutes before transferring them to a wire rack to cool completely.

Tips for Making Anzac Biscuits:

- **Golden Syrup:** Golden syrup is traditional in Anzac biscuits and gives them their distinct flavor. If you can't find golden syrup, you can use honey or corn syrup as a substitute.
- **Storage:** Store Anzac biscuits in an airtight container at room temperature. They will keep well for up to a week.
- **Variations:** Some variations include adding chopped nuts or chocolate chips to the mixture before baking for extra flavor and texture.

Enjoy these Anzac biscuits with a cup of tea or coffee as a delightful snack or treat, and remember their historical significance as you enjoy their delicious taste.

Lamingtons

Ingredients:

For the Sponge Cake:

- 1 cup all-purpose flour
- 1 tsp baking powder
- 1/4 tsp salt
- 1/2 cup unsalted butter, softened
- 3/4 cup granulated sugar
- 2 large eggs
- 1 tsp vanilla extract
- 1/2 cup milk

For the Chocolate Icing:

- 3 cups icing sugar (powdered sugar)
- 1/4 cup cocoa powder
- 1 tbsp unsalted butter, melted
- 1/2 cup milk, approximately
- 3 cups desiccated coconut, for coating

Instructions:

1. **Preheat Oven and Prepare Pan:**
   - Preheat your oven to 180°C (350°F). Grease and line a 9x9-inch square baking pan with parchment paper, leaving an overhang for easy removal.
2. **Make the Sponge Cake:**
   - In a medium bowl, sift together the flour, baking powder, and salt. Set aside.
   - In a large bowl, cream together the softened butter and sugar until light and fluffy.
   - Add the eggs, one at a time, beating well after each addition. Stir in the vanilla extract.
   - Gradually add the flour mixture to the creamed mixture, alternating with the milk. Begin and end with the flour mixture, mixing until just combined after each addition.
   - Pour the batter into the prepared baking pan and spread it out evenly.
3. **Bake the Sponge Cake:**
   - Bake in the preheated oven for 25-30 minutes, or until a toothpick inserted into the center comes out clean.
   - Remove the cake from the oven and allow it to cool in the pan for 10 minutes. Then, transfer it to a wire rack to cool completely.
4. **Prepare the Chocolate Icing:**
   - In a large bowl, sift together the icing sugar and cocoa powder.

- Add the melted butter and enough milk to make a smooth, pourable icing. The icing should be thick enough to coat the cake squares but thin enough to spread easily.

5. **Assemble the Lamingtons:**
     - Once the cake has cooled completely, trim the edges (if desired) and cut it into squares of equal size.
     - Place the desiccated coconut in a shallow bowl.
     - Dip each square of sponge cake into the chocolate icing, coating it completely. Allow any excess icing to drip off.
     - Immediately roll the coated cake square in the desiccated coconut, ensuring it is evenly coated on all sides.
     - Place the finished Lamingtons on a wire rack to set.
6. **Serve and Enjoy:**
     - Allow the Lamingtons to set for at least 1 hour before serving. They can be stored in an airtight container at room temperature for up to 3 days.

Tips for Making Lamingtons:

- **Sponge Cake Texture:** For a lighter texture, ensure not to overmix the cake batter.
- **Chocolate Icing Consistency:** Adjust the amount of milk in the icing to achieve a smooth and pourable consistency.
- **Variations:** Some variations include adding a layer of jam or cream between two cake squares before coating them with chocolate and coconut.

Lamingtons are a delightful treat that perfectly combines the flavors of chocolate and coconut. They are a favorite in Australia and are sure to be enjoyed by anyone who loves a sweet, indulgent dessert.

Sausage Rolls

Ingredients:

- 500g (1 lb) sausage meat (you can use pork, beef, or a mix)
- 2 sheets of ready-rolled puff pastry, thawed if frozen
- 1 small onion, finely chopped
- 1 garlic clove, minced
- 1/2 tsp dried thyme
- 1/2 tsp dried sage
- Salt and pepper, to taste
- 1 egg, beaten (for egg wash)

Instructions:

1. **Preheat Oven:**
   - Preheat your oven to 200°C (400°F) and line a baking sheet with parchment paper.
2. **Prepare the Filling:**
   - In a large mixing bowl, combine the sausage meat, finely chopped onion, minced garlic, dried thyme, dried sage, salt, and pepper. Mix until well combined.
3. **Assemble the Sausage Rolls:**
   - Cut each sheet of puff pastry in half lengthwise, so you have 4 long strips.
   - Divide the sausage meat mixture into 4 equal portions.
   - Spoon a portion of the sausage meat mixture along the center of each pastry strip, shaping it into a long sausage shape.
4. **Roll and Seal:**
   - Brush one edge of the pastry with beaten egg (this will help seal the roll).
   - Fold the pastry over the sausage meat and press the edges together to seal. Trim any excess pastry if necessary.
5. **Cut and Score:**
   - Cut each long roll into smaller sausage rolls, about 5-6 cm (2-2.5 inches) long.
   - Place the rolls seam side down on the prepared baking sheet. Score the tops of each roll with a sharp knife.
6. **Brush with Egg Wash:**
   - Brush the tops of the sausage rolls with beaten egg, which will give them a golden color when baked.
7. **Bake:**
   - Bake in the preheated oven for 20-25 minutes, or until the pastry is golden brown and crispy, and the sausage meat is cooked through.
8. **Serve:**
   - Remove from the oven and allow the sausage rolls to cool slightly before serving. They can be enjoyed warm or at room temperature.

Tips for Making Sausage Rolls:

- **Variations:** Add grated cheese, chopped herbs, or a dash of Worcestershire sauce to the sausage meat mixture for extra flavor.
- **Puff Pastry:** Ensure your puff pastry is thawed according to package instructions before using.
- **Storage:** Sausage rolls can be stored in an airtight container in the refrigerator for up to 3 days. They can also be frozen and reheated in the oven.

Sausage rolls are versatile and delicious, perfect for any occasion as a snack or light meal. They are sure to be a hit with family and friends!

Damper (Australian Soda Bread)

Ingredients:

- 3 cups self-raising flour
- Pinch of salt
- 1 cup water (approximately)
- Optional: 1/4 cup milk or 2 tbsp melted butter (for a softer texture)

Instructions:

1. **Preheat Oven:**
   - Preheat your oven to 200°C (400°F). Line a baking sheet with parchment paper.
2. **Mix Dry Ingredients:**
   - In a large mixing bowl, sift together the self-raising flour and a pinch of salt.
3. **Add Liquid Ingredients:**
   - Make a well in the center of the flour mixture and gradually add water (and milk or melted butter, if using) while stirring with a spoon or spatula. Mix until the dough comes together and forms a soft, slightly sticky ball. You may not need all of the water, so add it gradually.
4. **Knead the Dough:**
   - Turn the dough out onto a lightly floured surface and knead gently for a few minutes until smooth. Avoid over-kneading, as Damper benefits from a lighter touch for a more tender texture.
5. **Shape the Dough:**
   - Shape the dough into a round loaf, about 1-2 inches thick.
6. **Score the Dough:**
   - Use a sharp knife to score a cross or an "X" on the top of the loaf. This helps the heat penetrate the center of the bread while baking.
7. **Bake:**
   - Place the shaped Damper onto the prepared baking sheet.
   - Bake in the preheated oven for 30-35 minutes, or until the bread is golden brown and sounds hollow when tapped on the bottom.
8. **Cool and Serve:**
   - Remove from the oven and transfer the Damper to a wire rack to cool slightly before slicing and serving.

Tips for Making Damper:

- **Flavor Variations:** For a savory twist, you can add grated cheese, chopped herbs (like rosemary or thyme), or even dried fruits and nuts to the dough before baking.
- **Cooking Method:** Traditionally, Damper was cooked in the coals of a campfire. If you prefer, you can wrap the dough in foil and cook it on a grill or campfire for a rustic experience.

- **Storage:** Damper is best enjoyed fresh on the day it is made. If you have leftovers, store them in an airtight container and reheat before serving.

Damper is a versatile bread that can be served with butter, jam, honey, or even used as a base for savory toppings like cheese and sliced meats. It's a hearty and comforting bread that celebrates Australian culinary history and is easy to make with basic pantry ingredients.

Chia Pudding

Ingredients:

- 1/4 cup chia seeds
- 1 cup milk of your choice (almond milk, coconut milk, cow's milk, etc.)
- 1-2 tbsp maple syrup or honey (optional, for sweetness)
- 1/2 tsp vanilla extract (optional, for flavor)

Instructions:

1. **Mix Ingredients:**
   - In a bowl or a jar with a lid, combine the chia seeds, milk, maple syrup or honey (if using), and vanilla extract (if using). Stir well to combine.
2. **Let it Set:**
   - Let the mixture sit for about 5 minutes, then stir again to break up any clumps of chia seeds.
   - Cover the bowl or jar and refrigerate for at least 2 hours, or preferably overnight. During this time, the chia seeds will absorb the liquid and thicken to a pudding-like consistency.
3. **Stir and Serve:**
   - Before serving, give the chia pudding a good stir to redistribute the seeds. If it's too thick for your liking, you can stir in a little more milk until you reach the desired consistency.
4. **Top and Enjoy:**
   - Serve the chia pudding chilled, topped with your favorite fruits, nuts, seeds, or granola for added flavor and texture.

Tips for Making Chia Pudding:

- **Liquid Ratio:** The ratio of chia seeds to liquid is typically 1:4. Adjust the amount of milk based on how thick or thin you prefer your pudding.
- **Sweeteners:** You can adjust the sweetness of the pudding by adding more or less maple syrup or honey, or even using alternative sweeteners like agave syrup or stevia.
- **Flavor Variations:** Experiment with different flavors by adding cocoa powder for chocolate chia pudding, mashed fruits for fruity flavors, or spices like cinnamon or nutmeg for a warm, comforting taste.

Chia pudding is not only delicious but also packed with fiber, protein, and healthy fats from the chia seeds, making it a nutritious choice for breakfast or a satisfying snack. It's also vegan and gluten-free, catering to various dietary preferences.

Ricotta Hotcakes

Ingredients:

- 1 cup ricotta cheese
- 3/4 cup milk
- 2 large eggs, separated
- 1 tsp vanilla extract
- 1 cup all-purpose flour
- 1 tbsp granulated sugar
- 1 tsp baking powder
- Pinch of salt
- Butter or oil, for cooking

Instructions:

1. **Prepare the Batter:**
    - In a mixing bowl, combine the ricotta cheese, milk, egg yolks, and vanilla extract. Mix until smooth.
2. **Mix Dry Ingredients:**
    - In a separate bowl, sift together the flour, sugar, baking powder, and salt.
3. **Combine Wet and Dry Ingredients:**
    - Gradually add the dry ingredients to the ricotta mixture, stirring until just combined. Be careful not to overmix, as this can result in tough pancakes.
4. **Whip Egg Whites:**
    - In another clean bowl, beat the egg whites with a hand mixer or whisk until stiff peaks form.
5. **Fold in Egg Whites:**
    - Gently fold the beaten egg whites into the batter using a spatula. This will help create a lighter and fluffier texture.
6. **Cook the Hotcakes:**
    - Heat a non-stick frying pan or griddle over medium heat. Add a small amount of butter or oil to grease the pan.
    - Pour about 1/4 cup of batter onto the hot pan for each hotcake. Cook until bubbles form on the surface and the edges look set, about 2-3 minutes.
7. **Flip and Cook the Other Side:**
    - Carefully flip the hotcakes and cook for another 1-2 minutes, or until golden brown and cooked through.
8. **Serve:**
    - Serve the ricotta hotcakes warm, topped with your favorite toppings such as fresh berries, maple syrup, honey, or a dusting of powdered sugar.

Tips for Making Ricotta Hotcakes:

- **Consistency:** The batter should be thick but pourable. Adjust the amount of milk if needed to achieve the right consistency.
- **Cooking Temperature:** Cooking over medium heat ensures that the hotcakes cook through without burning on the outside.
- **Variations:** Add lemon zest or cinnamon to the batter for extra flavor, or fold in chocolate chips or blueberries for added sweetness.

Ricotta hotcakes are a delicious twist on traditional pancakes, offering a creamy texture and delightful flavor that makes them perfect for a special breakfast or brunch treat. Enjoy them with your favorite toppings and savor the fluffy goodness!

Corn Fritters

Ingredients:

- 1 cup fresh corn kernels (from about 2 ears of corn) or canned corn, drained
- 1/2 cup all-purpose flour
- 1/2 tsp baking powder
- 1/4 tsp salt
- 1/4 tsp black pepper
- 1/4 cup milk
- 1 large egg
- 2 green onions, finely chopped
- 1/4 cup finely chopped red bell pepper (optional)
- 2 tbsp chopped fresh herbs (such as parsley, cilantro, or basil)
- Oil, for frying (vegetable oil or canola oil)

Instructions:

1. **Prepare the Batter:**
   - In a large mixing bowl, combine the flour, baking powder, salt, and black pepper.
2. **Mix Wet Ingredients:**
   - In a separate bowl, whisk together the milk and egg until well combined.
3. **Combine Ingredients:**
   - Gradually add the milk and egg mixture to the dry ingredients, stirring until smooth.
   - Fold in the fresh corn kernels, chopped green onions, red bell pepper (if using), and fresh herbs. Mix until evenly distributed.
4. **Heat Oil:**
   - Heat a large skillet or frying pan over medium-high heat. Add enough oil to coat the bottom of the pan.
5. **Fry the Fritters:**
   - Once the oil is hot, drop spoonfuls of the batter into the skillet, using about 2 tablespoons of batter for each fritter. Flatten slightly with the back of the spoon.
6. **Cook Until Golden Brown:**
   - Fry the fritters for 2-3 minutes on each side, or until golden brown and crispy. Adjust the heat as needed to prevent burning.
7. **Drain and Serve:**
   - Remove the fritters from the skillet and drain on paper towels to remove excess oil.
8. **Serve Warm:**
   - Serve the corn fritters warm, optionally with a dollop of sour cream, salsa, or your favorite dipping sauce.

Tips for Making Corn Fritters:

- **Corn Variations:** Fresh corn kernels are best for flavor and texture, but you can also use canned corn kernels (drained well) or frozen corn (thawed and drained).
- **Additions:** Feel free to customize your corn fritters by adding ingredients like crumbled bacon, grated cheese, or diced jalapeños for a spicy kick.
- **Make Ahead:** You can prepare the batter ahead of time and fry the fritters just before serving for freshness and crispiness.

Corn fritters are a delicious way to enjoy fresh corn and make a fantastic addition to any meal or as a standalone snack. They're versatile, satisfying, and sure to be a hit with family and friends!

Beetroot and Sweet Potato Hash

Ingredients:

- 2 medium sweet potatoes, peeled and diced
- 2 medium beetroots, peeled and diced
- 1 small onion, finely chopped
- 2 garlic cloves, minced
- 2 tbsp olive oil
- 1 tsp dried thyme (or use fresh thyme leaves)
- Salt and pepper, to taste
- Optional: chopped fresh parsley or green onions for garnish

Instructions:

1. **Prepare the Vegetables:**
    - Peel and dice the sweet potatoes and beetroots into small cubes. Ensure they are similar in size for even cooking.
2. **Cook the Vegetables:**
    - Heat olive oil in a large skillet or frying pan over medium heat. Add the chopped onion and minced garlic, and sauté for 2-3 minutes until softened and fragrant.
3. **Add Sweet Potatoes and Beetroots:**
    - Add the diced sweet potatoes and beetroots to the skillet. Season with dried thyme, salt, and pepper.
4. **Sauté and Cook:**
    - Cook the vegetables, stirring occasionally, for about 15-20 minutes or until the sweet potatoes and beetroots are tender and lightly caramelized. Adjust the heat as needed to prevent burning.
5. **Finish and Serve:**
    - Once the vegetables are cooked through and golden brown, remove the skillet from heat.
    - Serve the beetroot and sweet potato hash warm, garnished with chopped fresh parsley or green onions if desired.

Tips for Making Beetroot and Sweet Potato Hash:

- **Uniform Size:** Cutting the sweet potatoes and beetroots into small, even cubes ensures they cook evenly and quickly.
- **Variations:** Feel free to add other vegetables such as bell peppers, zucchini, or mushrooms for added flavor and texture.
- **Serve with:** This hash pairs well with fried or poached eggs on top for a complete meal, or as a side dish with grilled chicken or fish.

Beetroot and sweet potato hash is not only delicious but also packed with nutrients and vibrant colors that make it visually appealing. It's a versatile dish that can be enjoyed for breakfast, brunch, or even as a wholesome dinner option.

Australian Beef Sausage

Ingredients:

- 1 kg (about 2.2 lbs) beef mince (ground beef), preferably with some fat content for juiciness
- 1/4 cup breadcrumbs (optional, for texture)
- 1 small onion, finely chopped
- 2 garlic cloves, minced
- 1 tbsp Worcestershire sauce
- 1 tbsp tomato sauce (ketchup)
- 1 tsp dried mixed herbs (such as parsley, thyme, oregano)
- Salt and pepper, to taste
- Natural sausage casings (available from butcher shops or online) or use as bulk sausage meat

Instructions:

1. **Prepare the Ingredients:**
   - In a large mixing bowl, combine the beef mince, breadcrumbs (if using), chopped onion, minced garlic, Worcestershire sauce, tomato sauce, dried herbs, salt, and pepper.
2. **Mix Thoroughly:**
   - Use your hands or a spoon to thoroughly mix the ingredients together until well combined. Ensure the seasonings are evenly distributed throughout the meat.
3. **Stuff the Sausage Casings (Optional):**
   - If using natural sausage casings, soak them in warm water according to package instructions to soften.
   - Attach the casing to a sausage stuffer or piping bag fitted with a large nozzle. Fill the casing with the meat mixture, leaving space to tie off the ends and form individual sausages.
4. **Form Sausages:**
   - Twist or tie off the sausage casings at regular intervals to form links. Alternatively, shape the meat mixture into patties or roll into logs if not using casings.
5. **Cooking Options:**
   - Grill: Preheat a grill or barbecue to medium-high heat. Grill the sausages, turning occasionally, until browned and cooked through, about 15-20 minutes.
   - Pan Fry: Heat a large frying pan over medium heat. Add a drizzle of oil and cook the sausages, turning occasionally, until browned and cooked through, about 15-20 minutes.
   - Bake: Preheat the oven to 180°C (350°F). Place the sausages on a baking sheet lined with parchment paper and bake for 20-25 minutes, or until cooked through.
6. **Serve:**

- Serve the Australian beef sausage hot off the grill or pan-fried, paired with your favorite sides such as mashed potatoes, sautéed vegetables, or in a crusty bread roll with mustard and onions.

Tips for Making Australian Beef Sausage:

- **Variations:** Customize the seasonings to your taste. Some recipes include spices like paprika, cumin, or fennel seeds for added flavor.
- **Storage:** Store uncooked sausages in the refrigerator for up to 2 days or freeze for longer storage. Cooked sausages can be refrigerated for 3-4 days or frozen for up to 3 months.
- **Handling Casings:** If using sausage casings, handle them gently to avoid tears. Rinse the casings under cold water before using to remove excess salt and preserve.

Australian beef sausage is a versatile dish that can be enjoyed in various ways, from a classic barbecue staple to a hearty breakfast option. It's a delicious way to savor the flavors of quality beef with the convenience of sausage preparation.

Sautéed Spinach and Mushrooms

Ingredients:

- 200g (7 oz) spinach leaves, washed and dried
- 200g (7 oz) mushrooms, sliced (button mushrooms or cremini mushrooms work well)
- 2 cloves garlic, minced
- 2 tbsp olive oil or butter
- Salt and pepper, to taste
- Optional: pinch of red pepper flakes for a bit of heat
- Optional: freshly grated Parmesan cheese for serving

Instructions:

1. **Prepare the Ingredients:**
   - If the spinach leaves are large, you can roughly chop them. Slice the mushrooms thinly.
2. **Sauté Mushrooms:**
   - Heat 1 tablespoon of olive oil or butter in a large skillet or frying pan over medium-high heat.
   - Add the sliced mushrooms to the pan and sauté for 4-5 minutes, stirring occasionally, until they are golden brown and tender. Remove the mushrooms from the pan and set aside.
3. **Sauté Spinach:**
   - In the same pan, add the remaining tablespoon of olive oil or butter.
   - Add the minced garlic and sauté for about 30 seconds until fragrant.
   - Add the spinach leaves to the pan in batches if necessary, as they will wilt down quickly. Cook for 1-2 minutes, stirring gently, until the spinach is wilted.
4. **Combine and Season:**
   - Return the sautéed mushrooms to the pan with the spinach.
   - Season with salt, pepper, and red pepper flakes (if using). Stir to combine all the ingredients and heat through for another minute.
5. **Serve:**
   - Transfer the sautéed spinach and mushrooms to a serving dish.
   - Optionally, sprinkle with freshly grated Parmesan cheese before serving.

Tips for Sautéed Spinach and Mushrooms:

- **Garlic:** Adjust the amount of garlic according to your preference. It adds a lot of flavor to the dish.
- **Mushrooms:** Don't overcrowd the mushrooms in the pan while sautéing to ensure they brown nicely.
- **Variations:** You can add diced onions or cherry tomatoes for added flavor and texture. For a creamy twist, stir in a tablespoon of cream or cream cheese at the end of cooking.

Sautéed spinach and mushrooms are versatile and pair well with grilled chicken, steak, pasta, or as a topping for toast or baked potatoes. They're quick and easy to make, making them a perfect side dish for any meal. Enjoy the earthy flavors and nutrient-rich goodness of this dish!

Zucchini and Sweet Corn Fritters

Ingredients:

- 2 medium zucchinis, grated
- 1 cup sweet corn kernels (fresh, canned, or frozen and thawed)
- 1/4 cup all-purpose flour
- 1/4 cup cornmeal (or additional flour)
- 1/4 cup grated Parmesan cheese
- 2 green onions, finely chopped
- 2 cloves garlic, minced
- 2 eggs, beaten
- 1/2 tsp baking powder
- Salt and pepper, to taste
- Olive oil, for frying

Instructions:

1. **Prepare the Zucchini:**
    - Grate the zucchinis using a box grater or a food processor. Place the grated zucchini in a colander and sprinkle with salt. Let it sit for about 10 minutes, then squeeze out excess moisture using a clean kitchen towel or paper towels.
2. **Mix the Batter:**
    - In a large mixing bowl, combine the grated zucchini, sweet corn kernels, flour, cornmeal, Parmesan cheese, green onions, minced garlic, beaten eggs, baking powder, salt, and pepper. Mix until well combined.
3. **Cook the Fritters:**
    - Heat a non-stick frying pan or skillet over medium heat. Add a drizzle of olive oil to coat the bottom of the pan.
    - Spoon about 2-3 tablespoons of the batter onto the hot pan for each fritter, flattening slightly with the back of the spoon.
    - Cook the fritters for 3-4 minutes on each side, or until golden brown and crispy. Add more olive oil to the pan as needed between batches.
4. **Serve:**
    - Transfer the cooked zucchini and sweet corn fritters to a plate lined with paper towels to absorb excess oil.
    - Serve the fritters warm, optionally with a dollop of sour cream, salsa, or your favorite dipping sauce.

Tips for Making Zucchini and Sweet Corn Fritters:

- **Consistency:** Adjust the amount of flour or cornmeal if needed to achieve a batter that holds together well but is not too dry.

- **Flavor Variations:** Add herbs like parsley, dill, or basil for extra flavor. You can also spice it up with a pinch of chili flakes or paprika.
- **Make Ahead:** You can prepare the batter ahead of time and cook the fritters just before serving for the best texture and flavor.

Zucchini and sweet corn fritters are versatile and perfect for using up summer produce. They're crispy on the outside, tender on the inside, and bursting with flavor. Enjoy these fritters as a delightful addition to any meal or as a tasty snack!

Australian-Style Scones with Jam and Cream

Ingredients:

- 2 cups self-raising flour
- 1/4 cup caster sugar (superfine sugar)
- Pinch of salt
- 60g (1/4 cup) unsalted butter, chilled and cubed
- 2/3 cup milk, plus extra for brushing
- Jam (typically strawberry or raspberry)
- Thickened cream or whipped cream, to serve

Instructions:

1. **Preheat Oven:**
   - Preheat your oven to 220°C (425°F). Line a baking tray with parchment paper.
2. **Mix Dry Ingredients:**
   - In a large bowl, sift the self-raising flour. Add the caster sugar and a pinch of salt. Mix well to combine.
3. **Cut in Butter:**
   - Using your fingertips, rub the chilled butter into the flour mixture until it resembles fine breadcrumbs. This step can also be done in a food processor.
4. **Add Milk:**
   - Make a well in the center of the flour mixture and pour in the milk. Use a butter knife or spatula to gently mix until a soft dough forms. Be careful not to overwork the dough.
5. **Shape and Cut:**
   - Turn the dough out onto a lightly floured surface. Gently knead the dough a few times until smooth.
   - Pat the dough out to about 2.5cm (1 inch) thickness. Use a round cutter (about 5-6cm in diameter) to cut out scones. Press straight down without twisting to ensure they rise evenly.
6. **Bake:**
   - Place the scones onto the prepared baking tray, leaving a little space between each.
   - Brush the tops of the scones lightly with milk.
7. **Bake the Scones:**
   - Bake in the preheated oven for 10-12 minutes, or until the scones are risen and golden brown.
8. **Serve:**
   - Remove the scones from the oven and transfer to a wire rack to cool slightly.
   - Serve warm with your favorite jam and a dollop of thickened cream or whipped cream.

Tips for Perfect Scones:

- **Handling the Dough:** Be gentle when kneading and shaping the dough to ensure light and fluffy scones. Overworking the dough can result in tough scones.
- **Baking Time:** Keep an eye on the scones while baking. They should be lightly golden on top when done.
- **Variations:** For a fruity twist, add a handful of sultanas or dried cranberries to the dough before shaping.

Australian-style scones with jam and cream are best enjoyed freshly baked while still warm. They are a delightful treat for any occasion and perfect for sharing with friends and family over a cup of tea or coffee.

Pumpkin and Ricotta Pancakes

Ingredients:

- 1 cup pumpkin puree (cooked and mashed pumpkin)
- 1/2 cup ricotta cheese
- 2 large eggs
- 1/4 cup milk
- 1 tsp vanilla extract
- 1 cup all-purpose flour
- 2 tbsp brown sugar
- 1 tsp baking powder
- 1/2 tsp baking soda
- 1/2 tsp ground cinnamon
- 1/4 tsp ground nutmeg
- 1/4 tsp salt
- Butter or oil, for cooking
- Maple syrup, for serving
- Optional: chopped nuts, fresh berries, or whipped cream for garnish

Instructions:

1. **Prepare Pumpkin Puree:**
   - Cook and mash pumpkin until smooth. Alternatively, canned pumpkin puree can be used.
2. **Mix Wet Ingredients:**
   - In a large bowl, whisk together the pumpkin puree, ricotta cheese, eggs, milk, and vanilla extract until well combined.
3. **Combine Dry Ingredients:**
   - In another bowl, whisk together the flour, brown sugar, baking powder, baking soda, cinnamon, nutmeg, and salt.
4. **Combine Wet and Dry Ingredients:**
   - Gradually add the dry ingredients to the wet ingredients, stirring until just combined. Do not overmix; a few lumps are okay.
5. **Cook Pancakes:**
   - Heat a non-stick skillet or griddle over medium heat. Add a small amount of butter or oil to coat the surface.
   - Pour about 1/4 cup of batter onto the skillet for each pancake. Cook until bubbles form on the surface and the edges look set, about 2-3 minutes.
6. **Flip and Cook the Other Side:**
   - Carefully flip the pancakes and cook for another 1-2 minutes, or until golden brown and cooked through.
7. **Serve:**

- Serve the pumpkin and ricotta pancakes warm, drizzled with maple syrup and topped with optional chopped nuts, fresh berries, or whipped cream.

Tips for Making Pumpkin and Ricotta Pancakes:

- **Pumpkin Puree:** Make sure the pumpkin puree is well-drained to avoid excess moisture in the pancake batter.
- **Ricotta Cheese:** Use whole milk ricotta for a creamy texture. If the ricotta is watery, drain it in a fine-mesh sieve before using.
- **Flavor Variations:** Add a pinch of ground ginger or cloves for extra warmth, or stir in chocolate chips for a decadent twist.
- **Batch Cooking:** Keep cooked pancakes warm in a low oven (about 200°F) while you finish cooking the rest of the batch.

Pumpkin and ricotta pancakes are a delightful way to enjoy the flavors of fall and make a perfect breakfast or brunch treat. They're fluffy, flavorful, and sure to be a hit with family and friends!

Croissants with Ham and Cheese

Ingredients:

- 4 croissants, split in half lengthwise
- 8 slices of ham (such as Black Forest ham or honey ham)
- 4 slices of cheese (such as Swiss cheese or cheddar)
- Dijon mustard (optional)
- Butter, for spreading

Instructions:

1. **Preheat Oven:**
    - Preheat your oven to 350°F (175°C).
2. **Prepare Croissants:**
    - Split each croissant in half lengthwise to create a top and bottom.
3. **Assemble Croissants:**
    - Spread a thin layer of Dijon mustard on the bottom half of each croissant (if using).
    - Layer 2 slices of ham and 1 slice of cheese on each bottom half of the croissants.
4. **Close Croissants:**
    - Place the top halves of the croissants over the ham and cheese to close them.
5. **Butter and Bake:**
    - Lightly spread butter on the top of each croissant.
    - Place the assembled croissants on a baking sheet lined with parchment paper.
6. **Bake:**
    - Bake in the preheated oven for about 10-12 minutes, or until the croissants are warmed through and the cheese is melted.
7. **Serve:**
    - Remove from the oven and serve the croissants warm. They are delicious on their own or paired with a fresh salad or fruit.

Tips for Making Croissants with Ham and Cheese:

- **Variations:** Feel free to customize by adding sliced tomatoes, avocado, or spinach to the croissants for added flavor and freshness.
- **Cheese Options:** Experiment with different cheeses like Gruyere, mozzarella, or provolone depending on your taste preference.
- **Toasting Croissants:** If you prefer a crispier texture, you can toast the assembled croissants in a toaster oven or under the broiler for a few minutes until golden brown.

Croissants with ham and cheese are a classic combination that's sure to please. They're easy to assemble and bake, making them perfect for a quick and tasty breakfast or brunch treat. Enjoy the buttery flakiness of the croissant paired with the savory goodness of ham and melted cheese!

Breakfast Burrito

Ingredients:

- 4 large flour tortillas (burrito size)
- 6 large eggs
- 1/4 cup milk
- Salt and pepper, to taste
- 1 tbsp butter or oil
- 1 cup shredded cheddar cheese (or your favorite cheese)
- 1 cup cooked breakfast sausage or bacon, chopped (optional)
- 1 cup diced bell peppers
- 1/2 cup diced onion
- 1/2 cup salsa or pico de gallo (optional)
- Fresh cilantro, chopped (optional)
- Sour cream or guacamole, for serving (optional)

Instructions:

1. **Prepare the Fillings:**
   - In a large skillet, heat a drizzle of oil over medium heat. Add the diced bell peppers and onions. Sauté until softened and slightly caramelized, about 5-7 minutes. Remove from skillet and set aside.
2. **Cook the Eggs:**
   - In a bowl, whisk together the eggs, milk, salt, and pepper until well combined.
   - In the same skillet, melt butter over medium heat. Pour in the egg mixture and cook, stirring occasionally, until the eggs are scrambled and cooked through. Remove from heat.
3. **Assemble the Burritos:**
   - Warm the tortillas briefly in a microwave or skillet to make them pliable.
   - Divide the scrambled eggs evenly among the tortillas, placing them in the center of each tortilla.
4. **Add Fillings:**
   - Layer the cooked bell peppers and onions, shredded cheese, cooked sausage or bacon (if using), and salsa or pico de gallo (if using) over the scrambled eggs.
5. **Roll the Burritos:**
   - Fold in the sides of each tortilla, then roll up tightly from the bottom to enclose the filling.
6. **Serve:**
   - Serve the breakfast burritos immediately, whole or sliced in half. Optionally, garnish with chopped cilantro and serve with sour cream or guacamole on the side.

Tips for Making Breakfast Burritos:

- **Customize Fillings:** Feel free to add or substitute fillings such as black beans, diced tomatoes, spinach, or avocado.
- **Make Ahead:** You can prepare the filling components ahead of time and assemble the burritos when ready to serve or wrap individually and freeze for later use.
- **Storage:** Store leftover burritos wrapped tightly in foil or plastic wrap in the refrigerator for up to 3 days. Reheat in the microwave or oven before serving.

Breakfast burritos are versatile and perfect for a quick and filling morning meal. They can be easily customized to suit your preferences and are a great way to start the day with a satisfying and delicious bite!

Aussie Meat Pie

Ingredients:

For the Pastry:

- 2 1/2 cups all-purpose flour
- 1/2 tsp salt
- 1 cup unsalted butter, cold and cut into cubes
- 6-8 tbsp ice water

For the Filling:

- 1 tbsp olive oil
- 1 onion, finely chopped
- 2 cloves garlic, minced
- 500g (1 lb) ground beef or lamb
- 1/4 cup all-purpose flour
- 1 cup beef or vegetable broth
- 1 tbsp Worcestershire sauce
- 1 tbsp tomato paste
- Salt and pepper, to taste
- 1/2 cup frozen peas (optional)

For Assembly:

- 1 egg, beaten (for egg wash)

Instructions:

1. Prepare the Pastry:

- In a large bowl, whisk together the flour and salt.
- Add the cold cubed butter and cut it into the flour mixture using a pastry cutter or your fingertips until it resembles coarse crumbs.
- Gradually add ice water, 1 tablespoon at a time, mixing with a fork until the dough just begins to come together.
- Turn the dough out onto a lightly floured surface and knead gently until it forms a cohesive ball. Wrap the dough in plastic wrap and refrigerate for at least 30 minutes.

2. Make the Filling:

- Heat olive oil in a large skillet over medium heat. Add the chopped onion and cook until softened, about 5 minutes.
- Add minced garlic and cook for another minute until fragrant.

- Add ground beef or lamb to the skillet, breaking it up with a spoon, and cook until browned and cooked through.
- Sprinkle the flour over the meat mixture and stir well to combine. Cook for 1-2 minutes to cook off the raw flour taste.
- Gradually add the beef or vegetable broth, Worcestershire sauce, and tomato paste, stirring constantly until the mixture thickens and comes to a simmer.
- Season with salt and pepper to taste. Stir in frozen peas if using. Remove from heat and let the filling cool slightly.

3. Assemble the Pies:

- Preheat your oven to 200°C (400°F). Lightly grease a 12-cup muffin tin.
- Divide the pastry dough into two portions, one slightly larger than the other. Roll out the larger portion on a lightly floured surface until about 1/8-inch thick.
- Using a round cutter or a large glass, cut out 12 circles to fit into the muffin tin (slightly larger than the cups to allow for overhang).
- Press the dough circles into the bottom and sides of the muffin cups, leaving any excess hanging over the edges.
- Fill each pastry-lined cup with the cooled meat mixture, dividing it evenly among the cups.

4. Top and Bake the Pies:

- Roll out the remaining pastry dough and cut out 12 slightly smaller circles for the pie tops.
- Brush the edges of the pastry bases with beaten egg. Place the pastry tops over the filling and press the edges together to seal. Trim any excess dough.
- Brush the tops of the pies with beaten egg to create a golden brown finish.
- Use a sharp knife to make a small slit in the top of each pie to allow steam to escape during baking.
- Bake in the preheated oven for 20-25 minutes, or until the pastry is golden brown and the filling is hot and bubbling.

5. Serve:

- Remove the Aussie meat pies from the oven and let them cool in the muffin tin for a few minutes before carefully transferring them to a wire rack to cool completely.
- Serve warm, optionally with tomato sauce (ketchup) or Worcestershire sauce on the side.

Tips for Making Aussie Meat Pies:

- **Make-Ahead:** The pastry dough and filling can be made ahead of time and stored separately in the refrigerator for up to 2 days before assembling and baking the pies.

- **Freezing:** Fully assembled and baked pies can be frozen for up to 3 months. Reheat in the oven at 180°C (350°F) until heated through.
- **Variations:** Add diced mushrooms, carrots, or other vegetables to the filling for added flavor and nutrition.

Enjoy these homemade Aussie meat pies as a delicious and comforting meal, perfect for any occasion!

Baked Beans on Toast

Ingredients:

- 1 can (400g) of baked beans (such as Heinz)
- 4 slices of bread (white or wholemeal)
- Butter, for spreading
- Optional: grated cheese, chopped parsley, or sliced avocado for garnish

Instructions:

1. **Prepare the Toast:**
   - Toast the bread slices until golden brown. Spread butter on each slice while still warm.
2. **Heat the Baked Beans:**
   - Pour the baked beans into a saucepan or microwave-safe bowl. Heat gently on the stovetop or in the microwave until hot throughout.
3. **Assemble:**
   - Spoon the hot baked beans evenly over the buttered toast slices.
4. **Garnish (Optional):**
   - Sprinkle grated cheese over the beans and toast, if desired. Alternatively, garnish with chopped parsley or sliced avocado for added flavor and texture.
5. **Serve:**
   - Serve the baked beans on toast immediately while warm.

Tips for Making Baked Beans on Toast:

- **Toast Variations:** Use your favorite type of bread for the toast, whether it's white, wholemeal, or even sourdough.
- **Cheese:** For a richer flavor, sprinkle grated cheddar or mozzarella cheese over the beans and toast before serving.
- **Customization:** Add a dash of hot sauce or Worcestershire sauce to the beans for extra flavor, or top with a fried or poached egg for a heartier meal.

Baked beans on toast is a quick, satisfying dish that's perfect for breakfast, lunch, or even a light dinner. It's a staple comfort food that's easy to prepare and enjoyed by many around the world!

Cherry Ripe Slice

Ingredients:

For the Base:

- 200g (about 7 oz) plain sweet biscuits (such as digestive biscuits or graham crackers), crushed into fine crumbs
- 1 cup desiccated coconut
- 125g (about 1/2 cup) unsalted butter, melted
- 395g (14 oz) can sweetened condensed milk

For the Filling:

- 200g (about 7 oz) glace cherries, chopped
- 1 cup desiccated coconut
- 395g (14 oz) can sweetened condensed milk

For the Topping:

- 200g (about 7 oz) dark chocolate, chopped
- 1 tbsp vegetable oil

Instructions:

1. **Prepare the Base:**
   - Line a 20cm x 30cm (8in x 12in) baking pan with parchment paper.
   - In a large bowl, combine the crushed biscuits, desiccated coconut, melted butter, and sweetened condensed milk. Mix until well combined.
   - Press the mixture firmly and evenly into the prepared baking pan. Use the back of a spoon or spatula to smooth the surface. Place in the refrigerator to chill while preparing the filling.
2. **Make the Filling:**
   - In a separate bowl, combine the chopped glace cherries, desiccated coconut, and sweetened condensed milk. Mix until well combined.
   - Spread the cherry and coconut filling evenly over the chilled biscuit base. Use a spatula to smooth the surface.
3. **Prepare the Topping:**
   - Place the chopped dark chocolate and vegetable oil in a microwave-safe bowl. Microwave in 30-second intervals, stirring in between, until the chocolate is melted and smooth.
   - Alternatively, melt the chocolate and vegetable oil in a heatproof bowl set over a pot of simmering water (double boiler method).
4. **Assemble and Chill:**

- Pour the melted chocolate evenly over the cherry and coconut filling, spreading it to cover the entire surface.
- Return the Cherry Ripe Slice to the refrigerator and chill for at least 2 hours, or until the chocolate topping is set.

5. **Slice and Serve:**
    - Once set, lift the slice out of the pan using the parchment paper edges. Use a sharp knife to cut into squares or bars.
    - Serve chilled and enjoy!

Tips for Making Cherry Ripe Slice:

- **Storage:** Store Cherry Ripe Slice in an airtight container in the refrigerator for up to 1 week.
- **Variations:** Feel free to experiment with different types of chocolate or add a layer of chopped nuts to the filling for added texture.
- **Gluten-Free Option:** Use gluten-free biscuits or cookies to make this slice gluten-free.

Cherry Ripe Slice is a decadent and indulgent treat that's perfect for dessert tables, potlucks, or anytime you crave a sweet chocolatey treat with a hint of cherry and coconut flavor.

Caramel Slice

Ingredients:

For the Shortbread Base:

- 1 cup (125g) all-purpose flour
- 1/2 cup (60g) powdered sugar (icing sugar)
- 1/2 cup (115g) unsalted butter, cold and cut into cubes

For the Caramel Filling:

- 1/2 cup (115g) unsalted butter
- 1/2 cup (100g) granulated sugar
- 2 tbsp golden syrup or light corn syrup
- 1 can (14 oz / 397g) sweetened condensed milk

For the Chocolate Topping:

- 200g (7 oz) dark chocolate, chopped
- 1 tbsp vegetable oil or butter

Instructions:

1. **Preheat Oven and Prepare Pan:**
   - Preheat your oven to 350°F (180°C). Grease and line a 9x9 inch (23x23 cm) square baking pan with parchment paper, leaving some overhang for easy removal later.
2. **Make the Shortbread Base:**
   - In a large bowl, combine the flour and powdered sugar. Add the cold cubed butter.
   - Using your fingertips or a pastry cutter, rub the butter into the flour mixture until it resembles fine breadcrumbs and starts to come together.
   - Press the mixture firmly and evenly into the prepared baking pan.
   - Bake in the preheated oven for 15-20 minutes, or until lightly golden. Remove from the oven and let cool while you prepare the caramel filling.
3. **Prepare the Caramel Filling:**
   - In a medium saucepan, combine the butter, granulated sugar, golden syrup (or corn syrup), and sweetened condensed milk.
   - Stir over medium heat until the butter has melted and the sugar has dissolved.
   - Bring the mixture to a gentle boil, stirring constantly. Reduce the heat to low and simmer for 5-7 minutes, stirring continuously, until the caramel thickens and turns a golden caramel color.
4. **Pour Caramel over Shortbread Base:**

- Pour the hot caramel filling over the cooled shortbread base, spreading it evenly with a spatula.
- Allow the caramel layer to cool completely at room temperature. You can speed up this process by placing it in the refrigerator for about 1 hour until firm.

5. **Make the Chocolate Topping:**
    - In a heatproof bowl set over a pot of simmering water (double boiler), melt the chopped dark chocolate and vegetable oil (or butter) together until smooth and glossy. Alternatively, microwave in 30-second intervals, stirring in between, until melted.
6. **Finish and Chill:**
    - Pour the melted chocolate over the cooled caramel layer, spreading it evenly with a spatula.
    - Return the caramel slice to the refrigerator and chill for at least 2 hours, or until the chocolate topping is set.
7. **Slice and Serve:**
    - Once set, lift the caramel slice out of the pan using the parchment paper edges. Use a sharp knife to cut into squares or bars.
    - Serve chilled and enjoy!

Tips for Making Caramel Slice:

- **Storage:** Store caramel slice in an airtight container in the refrigerator for up to 1 week. It can also be frozen for longer storage.
- **Variations:** Add a sprinkle of sea salt over the chocolate topping for a salted caramel version, or sprinkle chopped nuts like almonds or pecans over the caramel layer before adding the chocolate.
- **Cutting:** For clean and neat slices, use a sharp knife dipped in hot water and wiped dry between cuts.

Caramel slice is a delightful treat that combines the richness of caramel, the crunch of shortbread, and the smoothness of chocolate, making it a favorite for dessert lovers everywhere.

Egg White Omelette

Ingredients:

- 4 egg whites
- Salt and pepper, to taste
- 1/4 cup diced vegetables (such as bell peppers, onions, spinach, mushrooms)
- 1/4 cup shredded cheese (optional)
- 1 tsp olive oil or cooking spray

Instructions:

1. **Separate the Eggs:**
   - Crack the eggs and carefully separate the egg whites from the yolks. You can do this by cracking the egg over a bowl and transferring the yolk back and forth between the shell halves, letting the white drip into the bowl.
2. **Whisk the Egg Whites:**
   - In a bowl, whisk the egg whites until they become frothy. Season with salt and pepper to taste.
3. **Prepare the Filling:**
   - Heat olive oil or cooking spray in a non-stick skillet over medium heat.
   - Add diced vegetables (bell peppers, onions, spinach, mushrooms, etc.) to the skillet and sauté until softened, about 2-3 minutes.
4. **Cook the Egg Whites:**
   - Pour the whisked egg whites into the skillet, tilting the pan to spread them evenly over the vegetables.
   - Allow the egg whites to cook undisturbed for a few minutes until the edges start to set.
5. **Add Cheese (Optional):**
   - Sprinkle shredded cheese over one half of the omelette, if desired.
6. **Fold and Serve:**
   - Using a spatula, gently fold one half of the omelette over the other to form a half-moon shape.
   - Continue to cook for another minute or so until the cheese melts (if using) and the egg whites are fully cooked through.
7. **Serve:**
   - Slide the egg white omelette onto a plate and serve immediately.

Tips for Making Egg White Omelette:

- **Vegetable Variations:** Feel free to customize the omelette with your favorite vegetables, such as tomatoes, zucchini, or even avocado slices.
- **Protein Options:** Add cooked chicken, turkey, or ham for extra protein.

- **Herbs and Spices:** Enhance the flavor with fresh herbs like parsley, basil, or chives, or spices like paprika or garlic powder.
- **Non-Stick Pan:** Using a non-stick skillet is essential to prevent the egg whites from sticking.

Egg white omelettes are a nutritious and protein-packed breakfast or brunch option that can be easily customized to suit your taste preferences. They are low in calories and fat, making them a healthy choice for those watching their diet.

Chocolate Lamingtons

Ingredients:

For the Sponge Cake:

- 1 3/4 cups (220g) all-purpose flour
- 1 1/2 tsp baking powder
- 1/4 tsp salt
- 1/2 cup (115g) unsalted butter, softened
- 3/4 cup (150g) granulated sugar
- 3 large eggs
- 1 tsp vanilla extract
- 1/2 cup (120ml) milk

For the Chocolate Icing:

- 3 cups (360g) powdered sugar (icing sugar)
- 1/3 cup (30g) cocoa powder
- 1 tbsp unsalted butter, melted
- 1/2 cup (120ml) milk
- 2 cups desiccated coconut, for coating

Instructions:

1. Prepare the Sponge Cake:

- Preheat your oven to 350°F (180°C). Grease and line a 9x13 inch (23x33 cm) baking pan with parchment paper, leaving some overhang for easy removal.
- In a bowl, sift together the flour, baking powder, and salt. Set aside.
- In another large bowl, cream the softened butter and granulated sugar together until light and fluffy.
- Add the eggs one at a time, beating well after each addition. Stir in the vanilla extract.
- Gradually add the flour mixture to the butter mixture, alternating with the milk, beginning and ending with the flour mixture. Mix until just combined.
- Pour the batter into the prepared baking pan and spread it evenly.
- Bake for 25-30 minutes or until a toothpick inserted into the center comes out clean.
- Remove the cake from the oven and let it cool completely in the pan.

2. Cut and Prepare the Lamingtons:

- Once the cake has cooled, lift it out of the pan using the parchment paper overhang and place it on a cutting board.
- Trim the edges of the cake (optional) and cut it into even squares or rectangles, about 2x2 inches (5x5 cm).

- Place the desiccated coconut in a shallow bowl or plate.

3. Make the Chocolate Icing:

- In a bowl, sift together the powdered sugar and cocoa powder.
- Add the melted butter and milk, and whisk until smooth and well combined. The icing should be thick but pourable.

4. Coat the Lamingtons:

- Using two forks or skewers, dip each cake square into the chocolate icing, allowing the excess icing to drip off.
- Immediately roll the coated cake square in the desiccated coconut until evenly coated.
- Place the coated Lamington on a wire rack to set. Repeat with the remaining cake squares and icing.

5. Serve and Store:

- Once the chocolate icing has set, transfer the Chocolate Lamingtons to a serving plate.
- Serve at room temperature and enjoy!

Tips for Making Chocolate Lamingtons:

- **Cake Consistency:** For best results, ensure the sponge cake is fully cooled before cutting and coating to prevent crumbling.
- **Icing Thickness:** Adjust the consistency of the chocolate icing by adding more powdered sugar for a thicker icing or more milk for a thinner icing.
- **Variations:** Some recipes include a layer of strawberry or raspberry jam between the cake layers before coating with chocolate and coconut.

Chocolate Lamingtons are a delightful treat with a perfect balance of chocolate, coconut, and sponge cake, ideal for afternoon tea or dessert. They are also a beloved Australian classic that's sure to please friends and family alike!

Sourdough Toast with Vegemite

Ingredients:

- Sourdough bread slices
- Butter, optional
- Vegemite

Instructions:

1. **Toast the Sourdough Bread:**
   - Slice the sourdough bread into desired thickness.
   - Toast the bread slices until golden brown and crispy.
2. **Spread Butter (Optional):**
   - If desired, spread a thin layer of butter over the hot toasted sourdough slices. This step is optional but adds richness to the toast.
3. **Spread Vegemite:**
   - Using a knife, spread a thin layer of Vegemite over the buttered or plain toasted sourdough slices. Start with a small amount and add more to taste.
4. **Serve:**
   - Serve the sourdough toast with Vegemite immediately while warm. Enjoy as a breakfast dish or a quick snack.

Tips for Making Sourdough Toast with Vegemite:

- **Vegemite Amount:** Vegemite has a strong flavor, so start with a small amount and adjust according to your taste preferences.
- **Butter vs. No Butter:** The addition of butter enhances the richness of the toast but is optional. Vegemite can also be spread directly on plain toasted sourdough slices.
- **Sourdough Bread:** Choose a good quality sourdough bread with a crusty exterior and soft interior for the best texture.
- **Variations:** Experiment with different types of bread, such as whole grain or rye, for added variety.

Sourdough toast with Vegemite is a quick and easy breakfast or snack that showcases the distinctive savory taste of Vegemite. It's a quintessential Australian food experience loved by many!

Aussie Breakfast Pizza

Ingredients:

Pizza Dough:

- 1 pound (450g) pizza dough, homemade or store-bought
- Cornmeal or flour, for dusting

Toppings:

- 1 cup shredded mozzarella cheese
- 4 slices bacon, cooked and chopped
- 4 large eggs
- 1 cup cherry tomatoes, halved
- 1 cup baby spinach leaves
- Salt and pepper, to taste
- Fresh parsley or chives, chopped (optional, for garnish)

Sauce:

- 1/2 cup tomato sauce or pizza sauce
- 1 tsp olive oil
- 1 garlic clove, minced
- Salt and pepper, to taste

Instructions:

1. **Preheat the Oven:**
    - Preheat your oven to the highest temperature setting (usually around 475-500°F or 240-260°C). If using a pizza stone, place it in the oven to preheat as well.
2. **Prepare the Pizza Dough:**
    - Dust a baking sheet or pizza peel with cornmeal or flour to prevent sticking.
    - Stretch or roll out the pizza dough into a round or rectangular shape to fit your baking sheet or pizza stone.
3. **Make the Sauce:**
    - In a small bowl, mix together the tomato sauce, olive oil, minced garlic, salt, and pepper. Spread the sauce evenly over the pizza dough, leaving a small border around the edges.
4. **Assemble the Pizza:**
    - Sprinkle the shredded mozzarella cheese evenly over the sauce.
    - Scatter the chopped bacon, cherry tomatoes, and baby spinach leaves over the cheese.
5. **Add the Eggs:**

- Carefully crack each egg onto the pizza, spacing them evenly apart. You can crack the eggs directly onto the pizza or crack them into a small bowl first and then gently slide them onto the pizza.
6. **Bake the Pizza:**
    - Transfer the pizza to the preheated oven and bake for 10-12 minutes, or until the crust is golden brown, the cheese is melted and bubbly, and the egg whites are set but the yolks are still slightly runny.
7. **Finish and Serve:**
    - Remove the pizza from the oven and let it cool for a few minutes.
    - Season with salt and pepper to taste. Garnish with chopped parsley or chives, if desired.
    - Slice the Aussie Breakfast Pizza and serve immediately while hot.

Tips for Making Aussie Breakfast Pizza:

- **Pizza Dough:** Use store-bought pizza dough for convenience or make your own homemade dough.
- **Egg Doneness:** Adjust the baking time based on how you prefer your eggs—longer for fully cooked yolks or shorter for runny yolks.
- **Variations:** Feel free to customize with additional toppings such as sliced mushrooms, bell peppers, cooked sausage, or even avocado slices after baking.
- **Presentation:** For a more rustic look, you can crack the eggs onto the pizza before baking without separating them first. This creates a sunny-side-up egg appearance once baked.

Aussie Breakfast Pizza is a flavorful and satisfying dish that's perfect for breakfast, brunch, or even dinner. It combines the best of both worlds—pizza and breakfast—and is sure to be a hit with family and friends!

Veggie Frittata

Ingredients:

- 8 large eggs
- 1/4 cup milk or cream
- Salt and pepper, to taste
- 1 tbsp olive oil or butter
- 1 small onion, diced
- 1 bell pepper (any color), diced
- 1 cup sliced mushrooms
- 1 cup baby spinach leaves
- 1/2 cup cherry tomatoes, halved
- 1/2 cup shredded cheese (such as cheddar, mozzarella, or feta), optional
- Fresh herbs (such as parsley, basil, or chives), chopped, for garnish

Instructions:

1. **Preheat the Oven:**
   - Preheat your oven to 350°F (175°C).
2. **Prepare the Vegetables:**
   - In a large oven-safe skillet or frying pan, heat olive oil or melt butter over medium heat. Add diced onion and cook until translucent, about 3-4 minutes.
   - Add diced bell pepper and sliced mushrooms to the skillet. Cook until the vegetables are softened, about 5-6 minutes.
   - Add baby spinach leaves and cherry tomatoes to the skillet. Cook for another 2-3 minutes until the spinach is wilted and tomatoes are slightly softened. Season with salt and pepper to taste. Remove from heat.
3. **Prepare the Egg Mixture:**
   - In a bowl, whisk together eggs, milk or cream, salt, and pepper until well combined.
4. **Assemble and Cook the Frittata:**
   - Pour the egg mixture evenly over the sautéed vegetables in the skillet. Gently stir to distribute the vegetables throughout the eggs.
   - Sprinkle shredded cheese evenly over the top of the frittata, if using.
5. **Bake the Frittata:**
   - Transfer the skillet to the preheated oven. Bake for 20-25 minutes, or until the frittata is set in the center and the top is lightly golden brown.
6. **Serve:**
   - Remove the frittata from the oven and let it cool for a few minutes. Sprinkle with chopped fresh herbs for garnish.
   - Slice the Veggie Frittata into wedges or squares and serve warm. Enjoy as a main dish for breakfast, brunch, or even a light dinner.

Tips for Making Veggie Frittata:

- **Vegetable Variations:** Feel free to customize the frittata with your favorite vegetables such as zucchini, broccoli, or asparagus. Just make sure to sauté firmer vegetables first before adding quicker-cooking vegetables.
- **Cheese:** The shredded cheese adds extra flavor and richness to the frittata. Use your preferred type of cheese or omit it for a dairy-free option.
- **Oven-Safe Pan:** Ensure your skillet or frying pan is oven-safe to avoid any issues when transferring it from stovetop to oven.
- **Make-Ahead:** Frittatas can be made ahead of time and stored in the refrigerator for a few days. Reheat slices in the microwave or enjoy cold.

Veggie Frittata is a wholesome and filling dish that's perfect for using up leftover vegetables and creating a nutritious meal any time of day. Adjust the ingredients to suit your taste preferences and enjoy a delicious homemade frittata!

Grilled Haloumi with Avocado

Ingredients:

- 1 block of haloumi cheese, sliced into 1/2 inch thick pieces
- 1 ripe avocado, sliced
- Olive oil, for grilling
- Fresh lemon juice, for drizzling
- Freshly ground black pepper, to taste
- Fresh herbs (such as parsley or cilantro), chopped, for garnish (optional)

Instructions:

1. **Prepare the Haloumi:**
   - Heat a grill pan or non-stick skillet over medium-high heat. Lightly brush or drizzle olive oil over the haloumi slices to prevent sticking.
   - Grill the haloumi slices for about 2-3 minutes on each side, or until golden brown grill marks form and the cheese is heated through.
2. **Assemble the Dish:**
   - Arrange the grilled haloumi slices and avocado slices on a serving platter or individual plates.
   - Drizzle the avocado slices with a little bit of fresh lemon juice to add brightness and prevent browning.
3. **Season and Garnish:**
   - Season the grilled haloumi and avocado with freshly ground black pepper to taste.
   - Optionally, sprinkle chopped fresh herbs over the dish for added flavor and presentation.
4. **Serve:**
   - Serve the Grilled Haloumi with Avocado immediately while the haloumi cheese is warm and melty.

Tips for Making Grilled Haloumi with Avocado:

- **Choosing Haloumi:** Look for high-quality haloumi cheese that is firm and suitable for grilling. Haloumi has a salty taste and a firm texture that holds up well to grilling.
- **Grilling:** Make sure your grill pan or skillet is hot before adding the haloumi slices. Grill the cheese until it develops nice grill marks and becomes slightly softened.
- **Avocado Ripeness:** Use ripe but firm avocados for best results. You want them to be creamy but still hold their shape when sliced.
- **Variations:** Feel free to customize this dish with additional ingredients such as cherry tomatoes, cucumber slices, or a drizzle of balsamic glaze.

Grilled Haloumi with Avocado makes for a satisfying appetizer, light lunch, or even a side dish paired with a salad. It's quick to prepare and showcases the delicious combination of flavors and textures. Enjoy this dish as a delightful addition to your meal repertoire!

Vegemite and Cheese Scrolls

Ingredients:

For the Dough:

- 2 cups (250g) self-raising flour
- 1/4 teaspoon salt
- 50g butter, chilled and cubed
- 3/4 cup (185ml) milk

For Filling:

- Vegemite, to taste
- 1 cup grated cheese (cheddar, mozzarella, or your favorite melting cheese)

Instructions:

1. **Preheat Oven and Prepare Baking Dish:**
   - Preheat your oven to 200°C (400°F). Line a baking tray with parchment paper.
2. **Make the Dough:**
   - In a large bowl, sift together the self-raising flour and salt.
   - Rub in the chilled cubed butter with your fingertips until the mixture resembles breadcrumbs.
   - Make a well in the center and pour in the milk. Stir with a knife until the mixture comes together into a soft dough.
3. **Roll Out the Dough:**
   - Turn the dough out onto a lightly floured surface. Knead gently until smooth.
   - Roll out the dough into a rectangle, about 1/4 inch (0.5 cm) thick.
4. **Spread with Vegemite and Cheese:**
   - Spread a thin layer of Vegemite evenly over the rolled-out dough.
   - Sprinkle the grated cheese evenly over the Vegemite layer.
5. **Roll Up the Dough:**
   - Starting from the long edge, tightly roll up the dough to form a log.
6. **Slice into Scrolls:**
   - Using a sharp knife, cut the log into 1-inch (2.5 cm) thick slices.
7. **Bake the Scrolls:**
   - Place the scrolls cut-side up on the prepared baking tray, leaving a little space between each scroll.
   - Bake in the preheated oven for 15-20 minutes, or until the scrolls are golden brown and the cheese is melted and bubbly.
8. **Serve:**
   - Remove from the oven and let cool slightly on a wire rack.
   - Serve warm and enjoy these delicious Vegemite and Cheese Scrolls!

Tips for Making Vegemite and Cheese Scrolls:

- **Cheese Variation:** Experiment with different types of cheese for varying flavors. Cheddar, mozzarella, or even a blend of cheeses work well.
- **Vegemite Amount:** Adjust the amount of Vegemite based on your preference for its salty flavor. Start with a thin layer and add more if desired.
- **Storage:** Vegemite and Cheese Scrolls are best enjoyed fresh out of the oven but can be stored in an airtight container once completely cooled. Reheat in the oven or microwave before serving.
- **Variations:** Add cooked bacon bits, sliced ham, or caramelized onions to the filling for added texture and flavor.

Vegemite and Cheese Scrolls are perfect for breakfast, brunch, or as a savory snack any time of day. They are easy to make and sure to be a hit with Vegemite lovers and cheese enthusiasts alike!Aussie BBQ Breakfast

Beef Sausage Rolls

Ingredients:

For the Filling:

- 500g (1 lb) ground beef (minced beef)
- 1 small onion, finely chopped
- 1-2 garlic cloves, minced
- 1/2 cup breadcrumbs
- 1 tbsp Worcestershire sauce
- 1 tbsp tomato sauce (ketchup)
- Salt and pepper, to taste
- 1-2 tsp dried herbs (such as thyme, oregano, or mixed herbs)
- 1 egg, beaten (for egg wash)

For the Pastry:

- 1 package of puff pastry sheets (usually comes with 2 sheets)
- Flour, for dusting

Instructions:

1. **Preheat Oven:**
   - Preheat your oven to 200°C (400°F) and line a baking sheet with parchment paper.
2. **Prepare the Filling:**
   - In a large bowl, combine the ground beef, finely chopped onion, minced garlic, breadcrumbs, Worcestershire sauce, tomato sauce, salt, pepper, and dried herbs. Mix well until everything is evenly combined.
3. **Assemble the Rolls:**
   - Lay out one sheet of puff pastry on a lightly floured surface. Cut the sheet in half lengthwise to make two long strips.
   - Spoon the beef mixture lengthwise down the center of each strip of pastry.
4. **Roll the Pastry:**
   - Fold one side of the pastry over the filling and then fold the other side to overlap slightly, sealing the edges together. Press lightly to seal.
5. **Cut and Seal:**
   - Cut each long roll into smaller pieces, about 2-3 inches (5-7 cm) long.
   - Place the rolls seam-side down on the prepared baking sheet.
6. **Brush with Egg Wash:**
   - Brush the tops of the sausage rolls with beaten egg. This will give them a golden color when baked.
7. **Bake the Rolls:**

- Bake in the preheated oven for 20-25 minutes, or until the pastry is golden brown and the beef filling is cooked through.
8. **Serve:**
    - Remove from the oven and let cool slightly on a wire rack before serving.
    - Enjoy your homemade Beef Sausage Rolls warm or at room temperature.

Tips for Making Beef Sausage Rolls:

- **Pastry Handling:** Work quickly with the puff pastry to prevent it from becoming too warm and sticky. Keep any unused pastry covered with a damp cloth while working.
- **Variations:** Add grated cheese, diced vegetables (like carrots or bell peppers), or herbs of your choice to the beef filling for extra flavor and texture.
- **Make-Ahead:** You can assemble the rolls ahead of time and refrigerate them until ready to bake. They also freeze well—just freeze unbaked rolls on a baking sheet until solid, then transfer to a freezer bag. Bake from frozen, adding a few extra minutes to the baking time.

Beef Sausage Rolls are perfect for parties, picnics, or as a hearty snack. They are a favorite in Australia and are sure to be a hit wherever they're served!

Aussie BBQ Breakfast

Ingredients:

For the BBQ:

- Bacon rashers
- Beef sausages
- Thinly sliced steaks (such as sirloin or ribeye)
- Mushrooms, halved
- Tomatoes, halved
- Hash browns
- Olive oil or cooking spray

For the Eggs:

- Eggs (fried, scrambled, or poached)
- Salt and pepper, to taste
- Fresh herbs (optional, for garnish)

Accompaniments:

- Toast or bread rolls
- Butter or margarine
- Tomato sauce (ketchup)
- BBQ sauce
- Baked beans

Instructions:

1. **Prepare the BBQ:**
    - Preheat your BBQ or grill to medium-high heat. Ensure it is clean and lightly oiled.
2. **Cook the Meats and Vegetables:**
    - Cook the bacon rashers, beef sausages, and thinly sliced steaks on the BBQ until cooked to your liking. Turn occasionally for even cooking.
    - Grill the halved mushrooms and tomatoes until tender and lightly charred.
3. **Cook the Hash Browns:**
    - If using frozen hash browns, cook them on the BBQ according to package instructions. Alternatively, you can make homemade hash browns by grating potatoes, seasoning with salt and pepper, and frying until golden brown on both sides.
4. **Prepare the Eggs:**

- Cook the eggs on the BBQ. You can fry them in a pan or crack them directly onto the grill for a unique BBQ flavor. Alternatively, scramble the eggs in a pan on the BBQ.

5. **Assemble and Serve:**
   - Arrange the cooked meats, vegetables, eggs, and hash browns on a serving platter or individual plates.
   - Serve with toast or bread rolls, butter, tomato sauce, BBQ sauce, and baked beans on the side.
6. **Garnish and Enjoy:**
   - Season everything with salt and pepper to taste. Garnish with fresh herbs if desired.

Tips for Aussie BBQ Breakfast:

- **Variety:** Offer a variety of meats and vegetables to cater to different tastes. You can also include grilled onions or bell peppers for added flavor.
- **Cooking Time:** Be mindful of cooking times for different items on the BBQ. Start with meats that require longer cooking times and finish with quicker-cooking vegetables and eggs.
- **Customization:** Let guests customize their breakfast with their favorite condiments and sauces.
- **Outdoor Dining:** Enjoy your Aussie BBQ Breakfast outdoors with family and friends. It's perfect for weekend gatherings or special occasions.

An Aussie BBQ Breakfast is a fantastic way to start the day with a hearty and satisfying meal cooked over the BBQ. It captures the essence of Australian outdoor dining and is sure to be a memorable culinary experience!

Banana Bread with Macadamia Nuts

Ingredients:

- 2 cups all-purpose flour
- 1 teaspoon baking powder
- 1/2 teaspoon baking soda
- 1/2 teaspoon salt
- 1/2 cup unsalted butter, softened
- 3/4 cup granulated sugar
- 2 large eggs
- 3 ripe bananas, mashed
- 1/3 cup plain yogurt or sour cream
- 1 teaspoon vanilla extract
- 1 cup chopped macadamia nuts

Instructions:

1. **Preheat Oven and Prepare Pan:**
   - Preheat your oven to 350°F (175°C). Grease a 9x5-inch loaf pan or line it with parchment paper.
2. **Prepare Dry Ingredients:**
   - In a medium bowl, whisk together the flour, baking powder, baking soda, and salt. Set aside.
3. **Cream Butter and Sugar:**
   - In a large bowl, using a hand mixer or stand mixer, cream together the softened butter and granulated sugar until light and fluffy.
4. **Add Eggs and Wet Ingredients:**
   - Beat in the eggs one at a time until well combined. Mix in the mashed bananas, plain yogurt or sour cream, and vanilla extract until smooth.
5. **Combine Wet and Dry Ingredients:**
   - Gradually add the dry ingredients to the wet ingredients, mixing until just combined. Do not overmix.
6. **Fold in Macadamia Nuts:**
   - Gently fold in the chopped macadamia nuts into the batter until evenly distributed.
7. **Bake:**
   - Pour the batter into the prepared loaf pan, spreading it evenly.
   - Bake in the preheated oven for 60-70 minutes, or until a toothpick inserted into the center comes out clean or with a few moist crumbs attached.
8. **Cool and Serve:**
   - Allow the banana bread to cool in the pan for 10-15 minutes, then transfer it to a wire rack to cool completely before slicing.

Tips for Making Banana Bread with Macadamia Nuts:

- **Ripe Bananas:** Use ripe bananas with brown spots for the best flavor and sweetness.
- **Nuts:** Feel free to toast the macadamia nuts lightly before adding them to the batter for a richer flavor.
- **Storage:** Store the cooled banana bread in an airtight container at room temperature for up to 3 days, or wrap it tightly and freeze for up to 3 months.
- **Variations:** You can add a sprinkle of cinnamon or nutmeg for extra warmth in flavor. You can also drizzle the top with a simple glaze made of powdered sugar and milk if desired.

This Banana Bread with Macadamia Nuts is perfect for breakfast, brunch, or as a snack. It's moist, flavorful, and a wonderful way to use up ripe bananas. Enjoy your baking!

Salted Caramel Tim Tam Slice

Ingredients:

For the Base:

- 300g (10.5 oz) Arnott's Tim Tam biscuits (or any chocolate-coated biscuits)
- 100g (3.5 oz) unsalted butter, melted

For the Salted Caramel Filling:

- 1 can (395g / 14 oz) sweetened condensed milk
- 100g (3.5 oz) unsalted butter
- 2 tablespoons golden syrup or corn syrup
- 1/2 teaspoon sea salt flakes (adjust to taste)

For the Chocolate Topping:

- 200g (7 oz) dark chocolate, chopped
- 1 tablespoon vegetable oil or coconut oil

Instructions:

1. **Prepare the Base:**
   - Grease and line a 20cm x 20cm (8x8 inch) square baking tin with parchment paper, leaving overhang for easy removal later.
   - Crush the Tim Tam biscuits into fine crumbs using a food processor or place them in a zip-lock bag and crush with a rolling pin.
   - Mix the melted butter into the crushed Tim Tam crumbs until well combined.
   - Press the mixture evenly into the prepared baking tin. Use the back of a spoon or a spatula to compact it firmly. Chill in the refrigerator while you prepare the caramel filling.
2. **Make the Salted Caramel Filling:**
   - In a medium saucepan, combine the sweetened condensed milk, unsalted butter, and golden syrup (or corn syrup) over medium heat.
   - Stir continuously until the butter has melted and the mixture is smooth.
   - Bring to a gentle boil, then reduce the heat to low and simmer, stirring constantly, for about 5-7 minutes or until the caramel thickens and turns a golden brown color.
   - Remove from heat and stir in the sea salt flakes. Taste and adjust saltiness if needed.
   - Pour the salted caramel filling over the chilled Tim Tam base, spreading it evenly with a spatula. Return to the refrigerator to set while you prepare the chocolate topping.
3. **Prepare the Chocolate Topping:**

- In a heatproof bowl set over a pot of simmering water (double boiler method), melt the dark chocolate and vegetable oil (or coconut oil), stirring until smooth and combined.
- Alternatively, melt the chocolate in the microwave in short bursts, stirring in between each burst to ensure it melts evenly.

4. **Assemble the Slice:**
    - Pour the melted chocolate over the salted caramel layer, spreading it out evenly with a spatula to cover the entire surface.
    - Return the slice to the refrigerator and chill for at least 2 hours, or until the chocolate is completely set.

5. **Slice and Serve:**
    - Once set, remove the slice from the baking tin using the overhanging parchment paper. Use a sharp knife to cut into squares or rectangles.
    - Serve chilled and enjoy your Salted Caramel Tim Tam Slice!

Tips for Making Salted Caramel Tim Tam Slice:

- **Tim Tam Variation:** You can use different flavors of Tim Tam biscuits for a variation in taste. Classic, dark chocolate, or caramel flavors work well.
- **Storage:** Store the slice in an airtight container in the refrigerator for up to 1 week. It can also be frozen for up to 1 month. Allow to thaw in the refrigerator before serving.
- **Salt Adjustment:** Adjust the amount of sea salt flakes in the caramel filling to suit your taste preferences. Start with a smaller amount and add more if desired.

This Salted Caramel Tim Tam Slice is decadent, with layers of chocolatey biscuit base, gooey salted caramel, and rich dark chocolate topping. It's perfect for special occasions or as a delightful treat any time!

Lemon Myrtle and Aniseed Myrtle Granola

Ingredients:

- 3 cups rolled oats
- 1 cup mixed nuts and seeds (such as almonds, cashews, pumpkin seeds, sunflower seeds)
- 1/2 cup shredded coconut (optional)
- 1/4 cup coconut oil, melted
- 1/4 cup honey or maple syrup
- 1 tablespoon ground lemon myrtle
- 1 tablespoon ground aniseed myrtle
- 1/2 teaspoon salt
- 1/2 cup dried fruits (such as raisins, cranberries, or apricots), optional

Instructions:

1. **Preheat and Prepare:**
   - Preheat your oven to 325°F (160°C). Line a baking sheet with parchment paper or a silicone baking mat.
2. **Mix Dry Ingredients:**
   - In a large bowl, combine the rolled oats, mixed nuts and seeds, shredded coconut (if using), ground lemon myrtle, ground aniseed myrtle, and salt. Stir well to combine.
3. **Add Wet Ingredients:**
   - In a small saucepan, melt the coconut oil over low heat. Once melted, remove from heat and stir in the honey or maple syrup until well combined.
4. **Combine and Coat:**
   - Pour the melted coconut oil and honey/maple syrup mixture over the dry ingredients. Stir thoroughly until the oats and nuts are evenly coated.
5. **Bake:**
   - Spread the granola mixture evenly onto the prepared baking sheet. Press it down slightly with a spatula to create an even layer.
   - Bake in the preheated oven for 20-25 minutes, stirring halfway through, until the granola is golden brown and crisp.
6. **Cool and Add Dried Fruits:**
   - Remove the granola from the oven and let it cool completely on the baking sheet. Stir in the dried fruits, if using.
7. **Store:**
   - Once completely cooled, transfer the granola to an airtight container or glass jar for storage. It will keep well at room temperature for up to 2 weeks.

Tips for Making Lemon Myrtle and Aniseed Myrtle Granola:

- **Customization:** Feel free to customize the nuts, seeds, and dried fruits based on your preferences.
- **Myrtle Leaves:** If you have whole lemon myrtle and aniseed myrtle leaves, you can grind them into a powder using a spice grinder or mortar and pestle.
- **Sweetness:** Adjust the amount of honey or maple syrup to your desired level of sweetness.
- **Serving Suggestions:** Enjoy your Lemon Myrtle and Aniseed Myrtle Granola with yogurt, milk, or as a topping for smoothie bowls.

This granola not only provides a delicious crunch but also introduces the unique flavors of lemon myrtle and aniseed myrtle, showcasing the diversity of Australian native ingredients.

Aussie Bacon and Egg Pie

Ingredients:

- 1 sheet of pre-made shortcrust pastry, thawed if frozen
- 6 slices of bacon, diced
- 6 large eggs
- 1/2 cup heavy cream or milk
- Salt and pepper, to taste
- Fresh chives or parsley, chopped (optional, for garnish)

Instructions:

1. **Preheat Oven:**
   - Preheat your oven to 375°F (190°C). Grease a 9-inch pie dish or line it with parchment paper.
2. **Prepare Pastry:**
   - Roll out the shortcrust pastry on a lightly floured surface to fit your pie dish. Press the pastry into the dish, trimming any excess around the edges with a knife.
3. **Cook Bacon:**
   - In a skillet over medium heat, cook the diced bacon until crispy. Remove from heat and drain excess fat on paper towels.
4. **Prepare Egg Mixture:**
   - In a bowl, whisk together the eggs and heavy cream or milk until well combined. Season with salt and pepper to taste.
5. **Assemble Pie:**
   - Spread the cooked bacon evenly over the bottom of the pastry-lined pie dish.
   - Pour the egg mixture over the bacon.
6. **Bake:**
   - Place the pie dish in the preheated oven and bake for 25-30 minutes, or until the filling is set and the top is golden brown.
7. **Cool and Serve:**
   - Remove the pie from the oven and let it cool in the dish for 5-10 minutes before slicing.
   - Garnish with chopped fresh chives or parsley, if desired.

Tips for Making Aussie Bacon and Egg Pie:

- **Variations:** Add grated cheese, diced vegetables (such as bell peppers or spinach), or herbs to the egg mixture for added flavor and texture.
- **Pastry Options:** You can use puff pastry instead of shortcrust pastry for a flakier crust.
- **Make Ahead:** This pie can be made ahead of time and reheated in the oven before serving. It also makes a great leftover meal for breakfast or brunch.

- **Serving Suggestions:** Serve slices of the Aussie Bacon and Egg Pie warm or at room temperature with a side salad or roasted vegetables.

This Aussie Bacon and Egg Pie is perfect for any meal of the day, from breakfast to brunch or even a light dinner. It's hearty, flavorful, and sure to be a hit with family and friends!

Aussie Hash Browns

Ingredients:

- 4 medium potatoes, peeled and grated
- 1 small onion, finely chopped (optional)
- 2 tablespoons all-purpose flour
- 1 teaspoon salt
- 1/2 teaspoon black pepper
- Vegetable oil, for frying

Instructions:

1. **Prepare Potatoes:**
   - Peel the potatoes and grate them using a box grater or a food processor with a grating attachment. Place the grated potatoes in a large bowl of cold water for a few minutes to remove excess starch. Drain well and pat dry using paper towels or a clean kitchen towel.
2. **Mix Ingredients:**
   - In a large mixing bowl, combine the grated potatoes, chopped onion (if using), flour, salt, and black pepper. Mix well until everything is evenly distributed.
3. **Form Patties:**
   - Heat a large skillet or frying pan over medium heat and add enough vegetable oil to coat the bottom of the pan.
   - Take a handful of the potato mixture and shape it into a compact patty or cake, about 1/2 inch thick. Repeat with the remaining mixture, placing the patties in the hot oil.
4. **Fry Hash Browns:**
   - Cook the hash browns in batches to avoid overcrowding the pan. Fry each patty for about 3-4 minutes on each side, or until golden brown and crispy. Use a spatula to gently flip them over halfway through cooking.
5. **Drain and Serve:**
   - Once cooked, transfer the hash browns to a plate lined with paper towels to drain excess oil.
6. **Serve:**
   - Serve the Aussie Hash Browns hot as a side dish with breakfast eggs, bacon, or sausages. They also pair well with a dollop of sour cream or ketchup on the side.

Tips for Making Aussie Hash Browns:

- **Potato Texture:** For crispy hash browns, ensure the grated potatoes are well drained and dried before mixing with other ingredients.
- **Seasoning:** Adjust the amount of salt and pepper according to your taste preferences.

- **Cooking Oil:** Use enough vegetable oil to cover the bottom of the skillet but not too much to deep fry the hash browns. You want them to crisp up evenly.
- **Variations:** Add grated cheese, herbs (such as parsley or chives), or spices (like paprika or garlic powder) to the potato mixture for extra flavor.

These Aussie Hash Browns are simple to make and provide a delicious addition to any breakfast or brunch spread. Enjoy their crispy exterior and fluffy interior with your favorite morning dishes!

Aussie Weet-Bix Slice

Ingredients:

For the Base:

- 4 Weet-Bix biscuits, crushed (about 1 cup)
- 1 cup rolled oats
- 1/2 cup desiccated coconut
- 1/2 cup brown sugar, firmly packed
- 150g (5.3 oz) unsalted butter, melted

For the Topping:

- 1 cup icing sugar (powdered sugar)
- 2 tablespoons cocoa powder
- 1 tablespoon butter, softened
- 2 tablespoons hot water
- Desiccated coconut, for sprinkling (optional)

Instructions:

1. **Preheat Oven:**
   - Preheat your oven to 180°C (350°F). Grease and line a 20cm x 30cm (8x12 inch) baking dish with parchment paper, leaving overhang for easy removal.
2. **Prepare the Base:**
   - In a large mixing bowl, combine the crushed Weet-Bix biscuits, rolled oats, desiccated coconut, and brown sugar.
   - Pour the melted butter over the dry ingredients and mix until well combined and the mixture resembles coarse crumbs.
3. **Press into Pan:**
   - Press the mixture firmly and evenly into the prepared baking dish using the back of a spoon or your fingertips.
4. **Bake the Base:**
   - Bake in the preheated oven for 15-20 minutes, or until lightly golden. Remove from the oven and let it cool slightly while preparing the topping.
5. **Make the Topping:**
   - In a medium bowl, sift together the icing sugar and cocoa powder.
   - Add the softened butter and hot water to the dry ingredients. Mix until smooth and well combined.
6. **Spread Topping:**
   - Spread the chocolate topping evenly over the warm base using a spatula or the back of a spoon. Work quickly as the topping will set.
7. **Chill and Set:**

- Sprinkle desiccated coconut over the chocolate topping, if using. Place the slice in the refrigerator to chill and allow the topping to set completely, about 1-2 hours.
8. **Slice and Serve:**
    - Once set, lift the slice out of the baking dish using the parchment paper overhang. Cut into squares or bars using a sharp knife.

Tips for Making Aussie Weet-Bix Slice:

- **Variations:** You can add chopped nuts, dried fruit (such as raisins or cranberries), or even chocolate chips to the base mixture for extra flavor and texture.
- **Storage:** Store the Weet-Bix Slice in an airtight container in the refrigerator for up to one week. It can also be frozen for longer storage.
- **Cutting:** To get clean slices, run a knife under hot water before each cut and wipe it dry.

This Aussie Weet-Bix Slice is a delicious treat that combines the wholesome crunch of Weet-Bix with a rich chocolate topping, making it perfect for morning or afternoon tea!

Aussie Pumpkin Bread

Ingredients:

- 1 3/4 cups all-purpose flour
- 1 teaspoon baking soda
- 1/2 teaspoon baking powder
- 1/2 teaspoon salt
- 1 teaspoon ground cinnamon
- 1/2 teaspoon ground ginger
- 1/4 teaspoon ground nutmeg
- 1/4 teaspoon ground cloves
- 1 cup pumpkin puree (canned or homemade)
- 1/2 cup vegetable oil or melted butter
- 1 cup granulated sugar
- 1/2 cup brown sugar, packed
- 2 large eggs
- 1 teaspoon vanilla extract
- 1/2 cup chopped walnuts or pecans (optional)

Instructions:

1. **Preheat Oven and Prepare Pan:**
   - Preheat your oven to 350°F (175°C). Grease and flour a 9x5-inch loaf pan, or line it with parchment paper for easy removal.
2. **Mix Dry Ingredients:**
   - In a medium bowl, whisk together the flour, baking soda, baking powder, salt, cinnamon, ginger, nutmeg, and cloves until well combined. Set aside.
3. **Combine Wet Ingredients:**
   - In a large bowl, whisk together the pumpkin puree, vegetable oil (or melted butter), granulated sugar, brown sugar, eggs, and vanilla extract until smooth and well combined.
4. **Combine and Fold:**
   - Gradually add the dry ingredients to the wet ingredients, stirring with a spatula or wooden spoon until just combined. Do not overmix. If using nuts, fold them into the batter.
5. **Bake:**
   - Pour the batter into the prepared loaf pan and smooth the top with a spatula.
   - Bake in the preheated oven for 60-70 minutes, or until a toothpick inserted into the center of the bread comes out clean or with a few moist crumbs.
6. **Cool and Serve:**
   - Allow the bread to cool in the pan for 10 minutes before transferring it to a wire rack to cool completely.
7. **Slice and Enjoy:**

- Once cooled, slice the Aussie Pumpkin Bread and serve. It's delicious on its own or with a spread of butter.

Tips for Making Aussie Pumpkin Bread:

- **Pumpkin Puree:** Use canned pumpkin puree or homemade pumpkin puree for this recipe. Make sure it's well-drained if homemade.
- **Spice Adjustment:** Adjust the spices according to your preference. You can increase or decrease the amounts of cinnamon, ginger, nutmeg, and cloves to suit your taste.
- **Add-Ins:** Feel free to add chopped nuts, chocolate chips, or dried fruit to the batter for added texture and flavor.
- **Storage:** Store the cooled pumpkin bread in an airtight container at room temperature for up to 3 days, or refrigerate for longer shelf life.

This Aussie Pumpkin Bread is moist, flavorful, and perfect for enjoying during breakfast, brunch, or as a tasty snack any time of day. The blend of spices and pumpkin creates a warm and comforting treat that everyone will love.

Aussie Gluten-Free Bread

Ingredients:

- 1 1/2 cups gluten-free all-purpose flour blend
- 1/2 cup almond flour
- 1/2 cup potato starch
- 1/4 cup tapioca flour/starch
- 2 teaspoons baking powder
- 1 teaspoon baking soda
- 1 teaspoon salt
- 1 teaspoon xanthan gum (if your flour blend doesn't already contain it)
- 1/2 teaspoon ground cinnamon
- 1/4 teaspoon ground nutmeg
- 1/4 teaspoon ground ginger
- 3 large eggs
- 1/2 cup unsweetened applesauce
- 1/4 cup honey or maple syrup
- 1/4 cup olive oil or melted coconut oil
- 1 teaspoon vanilla extract
- 1 cup mashed ripe bananas (about 2 medium bananas)
- 1/2 cup chopped walnuts or pecans (optional)

Instructions:

1. **Preheat Oven and Prepare Pan:**
   - Preheat your oven to 350°F (175°C). Grease a 9x5-inch loaf pan or line it with parchment paper.
2. **Mix Dry Ingredients:**
   - In a medium bowl, whisk together the gluten-free flour blend, almond flour, potato starch, tapioca flour, baking powder, baking soda, salt, xanthan gum (if using), cinnamon, nutmeg, and ginger until well combined. Set aside.
3. **Combine Wet Ingredients:**
   - In a large bowl, whisk together the eggs, applesauce, honey or maple syrup, olive oil or melted coconut oil, and vanilla extract until smooth.
4. **Add Mashed Bananas:**
   - Stir in the mashed bananas until well incorporated into the wet mixture.
5. **Combine Wet and Dry Mixtures:**
   - Gradually add the dry ingredients to the wet ingredients, mixing until just combined. Do not overmix. If using, fold in chopped nuts.
6. **Bake:**
   - Pour the batter into the prepared loaf pan and smooth the top with a spatula.
   - Bake in the preheated oven for 50-60 minutes, or until a toothpick inserted into the center comes out clean or with a few moist crumbs.

7. **Cool and Serve:**
   - Allow the bread to cool in the pan for 10 minutes before transferring it to a wire rack to cool completely.
8. **Slice and Enjoy:**
   - Once cooled, slice the Aussie Gluten-Free Bread and serve. It's delicious on its own or toasted with a spread of butter or nut butter.

Tips for Making Aussie Gluten-Free Bread:

- **Flour Blend:** Use a good quality gluten-free all-purpose flour blend that is suitable for baking. If your blend doesn't contain xanthan gum, make sure to add it separately as indicated.
- **Bananas:** Use ripe bananas for the best flavor and sweetness. Mash them well before adding to the batter.
- **Storage:** Store the cooled bread in an airtight container at room temperature for up to 3 days, or slice and freeze for longer storage.
- **Variations:** You can add dried fruit, chocolate chips, or seeds to the batter for added texture and flavor.

This Aussie Gluten-Free Bread is moist, flavorful, and perfect for those who are avoiding gluten but still want to enjoy a delicious homemade loaf. It's a wonderful addition to any breakfast or brunch spread!

Aussie Zucchini Bread

Ingredients:

- 1 1/2 cups grated zucchini (about 1 medium zucchini)
- 1 cup all-purpose flour
- 1/2 cup whole wheat flour
- 1 teaspoon baking powder
- 1/2 teaspoon baking soda
- 1/2 teaspoon salt
- 1 teaspoon ground cinnamon
- 1/2 teaspoon ground nutmeg
- 1/4 teaspoon ground ginger
- 2 large eggs
- 1/2 cup brown sugar, packed
- 1/4 cup white granulated sugar
- 1/2 cup vegetable oil
- 1 teaspoon vanilla extract
- 1/2 cup chopped walnuts or pecans (optional)

Instructions:

1. **Prepare Zucchini:**
   - Grate the zucchini using a box grater. Place the grated zucchini in a clean kitchen towel and squeeze out excess moisture. Set aside.
2. **Preheat Oven and Prepare Pan:**
   - Preheat your oven to 350°F (175°C). Grease and flour a 9x5-inch loaf pan, or line it with parchment paper for easy removal.
3. **Mix Dry Ingredients:**
   - In a large mixing bowl, whisk together the all-purpose flour, whole wheat flour, baking powder, baking soda, salt, cinnamon, nutmeg, and ginger until well combined. Set aside.
4. **Mix Wet Ingredients:**
   - In another bowl, whisk together the eggs, brown sugar, granulated sugar, vegetable oil, and vanilla extract until smooth.
5. **Combine Wet and Dry Ingredients:**
   - Pour the wet ingredients into the bowl with the dry ingredients. Stir gently with a spatula or wooden spoon until just combined and no streaks of flour remain.
6. **Fold in Zucchini and Nuts:**
   - Gently fold in the grated zucchini and chopped nuts (if using) until evenly distributed throughout the batter.
7. **Bake:**
   - Pour the batter into the prepared loaf pan, spreading it evenly. Bake in the preheated oven for 50-60 minutes, or until a toothpick inserted into the center comes out clean.

8. **Cool:**
    - Allow the bread to cool in the pan for 10-15 minutes, then remove it from the pan and transfer to a wire rack to cool completely.
9. **Serve:**
    - Slice and serve the Aussie Zucchini Bread plain, with butter, or with a dollop of cream cheese.

Enjoy your delicious Aussie Zucchini Bread! It's perfect for breakfast, as a snack, or for afternoon tea.

Aussie Orange Marmalade

Ingredients:

- 4 large oranges (preferably Seville oranges for a more traditional bitterness)
- 2 lemons
- 6 cups water
- 6 cups granulated sugar

Instructions:

1. **Prepare the Fruit:**
   - Wash the oranges and lemons thoroughly. Cut them in half and squeeze out the juice into a large measuring cup or bowl. Set the juice aside.
   - Take the squeezed halves and cut them into very thin slices. Remove any seeds as you go.
2. **Cooking the Marmalade:**
   - In a large, heavy-bottomed pot, combine the sliced oranges, sliced lemons, and water. Bring the mixture to a boil over medium-high heat.
   - Reduce the heat to low and simmer gently, uncovered, for about 1 hour or until the fruit peel is very tender and translucent.
3. **Add Sugar:**
   - Add the sugar to the pot, stirring constantly until it is completely dissolved. Increase the heat to medium-high and bring the mixture to a rapid boil.
4. **Boil and Test for Doneness:**
   - Boil the mixture rapidly, stirring occasionally, for about 15-20 minutes or until the marmalade reaches the setting point. You can test the setting point by placing a small amount of marmalade on a chilled plate and letting it cool for a minute. It should wrinkle when pushed with a finger when ready.
5. **Skim and Rest:**
   - Skim off any foam that forms on the surface of the marmalade during boiling.
   - Remove the pot from the heat and let the marmalade sit for about 5-10 minutes to cool slightly and allow the fruit to distribute evenly.
6. **Jar and Store:**
   - Carefully ladle the hot marmalade into clean, sterilized jars, leaving about 1/4 inch of headspace. Wipe the jar rims clean with a damp cloth.
   - Seal the jars tightly with sterilized lids and bands.
7. **Cool and Store:**
   - Let the jars cool to room temperature, then store them in a cool, dark place. The marmalade will continue to thicken as it cools.
8. **Enjoy:**
   - Once cooled and set, enjoy your Aussie Orange Marmalade on toast, scones, or as a glaze for meats.

This recipe makes about 6-7 cups of marmalade. It's a delightful treat with a perfect balance of sweet and tangy flavors, typical of Aussie-style marmalades.

www.ingramcontent.com/pod-product-compliance
Lightning Source LLC
LaVergne TN
LVHW081607060526
838201LV00054B/2118